HEAVY IS THE CROWN

ONE WOMAN'S STORY OF THE STRENGTH IT TAKES TO MANAGE HER #QUEENDOM

ISBN: 9781798645338

First Printing: 2019

"Bulk purchase discounts, special editions, and customized excerpts are available direct from the publisher. For information about books for educational, business, or promotional purposes and more...
Submit all publisher requests to info@moniqueburks.com

D1518465

I want to dedicate this book to my mother Cynthia, my brother Charles, my family, my husband, my children, my father, and all the Queens out there.

About Monique Burks

Monique Burks is a fresh and entertaining motivational speaker, as well as an entertainer, mother, wife, entrepreneur, food fanatic and CEO of EmpowerHER network where she shows women who look good on the outside how to feel good on the inside.

As founder and CEO of EmpowerHer community, One of her many organization she is creating, Monique's goal is to be the best example of what a wife and mother looks like to everyone she comes across.

Monique's story begins in 2014 when her mother died of an brain aneurism and cardiac arrest from recurring brain tumors. Her world turned upside down as she started to drink heavily, depression, attempted suicide, anxiety, mild heart attack and PTSD. Even-though she is still enduring some of the issues, she still finds a way to move forward and survive.

She founded EmpowerHer because of how many women always confided in her strength and perseverance through her trying times. Monique wanted to help anyone who was going through loss of a love one, hopelessness, being alone, and giving up on life. She wanted to show them how she fights everyday to LIVE and keep moving in her daily life.

Monique lives in Dallas Texas area and plans on expanding outside of Texas. A leader, A inspiration, A power house and a Queen to her peers. I can only imagine what else she has to offer in the future.

CONTENTS

1

A Queens Beginning

Her name is Cynthia Marie McFadden-Roberts. She was born on October 28,1942 in a small town called Ozan, Arkansas not too far from Hope, Arkansas. Her parents are Clemon and Nancy Mcfadden. They owned a little house on a farm with no running water but they had a watering well. On the farm they had cows, hoggs, chicken, a garden, bails of hay which her father sold and a slaughterhouse. During winter they used the one big heater in the front of the house to stay warm. You see, they was poor but they made the best of what they had.

Everything was done on the farm. They had a little convenience store and a Piggly Wiggle but both were miles away. This town was small, I mean Ozan was so small you could blink and you had passed it.

My mom was the youngest of 6 children. Their where 4 girls and 2 boys. Faye, Carrie, Lou, Cynthia(my mom), Clemon Jr & Alfonso. My mom told
me they kept her close to the house and she hated it lol. While all of the other sibling got to go up on top of the hill mom had to stay home. Madea said there was too much going on up there that she was not old

enough to be a part of. You see this was like the club for them lol. They had baseball games, drinking, club house and other activities. Let's just say her siblings should have not been up there either but they manage to get away with more than mom.

Mom told me she got so mad one day because she could not go up on them hill that she burned down one of my grandfathers barns. She said they beat her ass for days lol. My mom the rebel but anyway mom always dreamed of moving to the big city Dallas, TX when she got older. She hated the farm life and wanted better for herself.

She moved to Dallas after graduating high school at the age of 16 and was living with her sister Carrie for a little while until she got her first job working at an optical eyeglass company. During this time she met my father Charles Roberts Sr. My dad told me he was walking by the eye glass shop saw my mom and said he had to have her, lol my dad said he was a pimp in his younger days. Well it must have worked because my dad and mother got married in 1967 which ironically my brother Charles Roberts Jr was born in the same year. Yes my mom was pregnant when her and my dad got married back in the 60's if you got a women pregnant you married her.

Then 5 years later I came in 1972 Monique Roberts with my premature lil self. Mom told me it was not easy for her and dad. It was really hard. They had one car, they stayed in the little apartment with 2 children a toddler and a baby. People would break in your apartments all the time and the rent was extremely high. My mom said it was hard to find people who wanted to babysit so that meant her and dad not getting out much like they use to which put a strain on the marriage but they pushed on to do what they could to take care of me and Charles. To help with child care my mom said aunt Carried introduced my mom to Aunt Mary that is the only name I remembered her by.

She was an old lady that lived in a house in South Dallas next to the old Kentucky fried chicken building which is now a Salon next to Lott's funeral home. If you from the D then you know where I'm talking about. She was a very nice lady. She had a cool house with a lot of antiques that she would not let us play with. There was the cabinet full of figurines and till this day we have that cabinet in our home. I finally got to touch them lol. We watched Tv, she did not cook much but she loved Kentucky fried chicken. We ate there almost everyday and my fat little butt did not mind but my mom hated it but Aunt Mary did not care. She was always fussing at my mom and dad about me and Charles but they didn't care they knew if they talked back they would not have a baby sitter. Aunt Mary loved us because she did not have any children so she loves us like we was hers.

Mom told me she help her and my dad get their first house because she new the people who was selling the house. Mom said that Aunt Mary bought me and Charles a bed and a dresser to put our clothes in. She told my mom and dad they had to get there own stuff for there room. The children should not have to suffer because they couldn't get it together. Damn my Aunt Mary was gangster. She did not play and said what was on her mind. Mom had the nerve to take one of our beds and put it in her and dads room. My Aunt Mary came over and made dad take it down and put to back in the room lol. She said, I told y'all I don't help grown ass men and women only the children. Take it down again and see what happen. Needless to say mom and dad bought a bed real fast. I loved that old lady and when she became sick and died that hurt my heart.

All I can remember is standing at the hearse crying as they took her away. I was very young but she left an impact on me that I will always remember.

Mom said dad started drinking a lot due to the stresses of being a young husband and father. The job was not making much money so the marital problems continued late night parting, arguing, drinking with the boys until it took a toll on both of them and they finally divorced 9 years later. My mom was left to raise 2 children on her own a 6 year old toddler and a 1 year old baby girl.

Mom knew she needed a better job so she went on the hunt for one. She ended up getting a job with Republic bank now knows as Bank of America. It was a good job but not enough so she picked up a part time job at Sanger Harris now know as Macy's. She worked both of these jobs to provide a good life for me and my brother Charles. I always admired her strength as a little girl. It seemed like nothing could stop her. She always made a way. We never went hungry or wanted for anything. I felt like my mom was invisible.

It was mom, me and Charles our happy little family until Her new dude came into the picture. My mom rarely dated because she did not want just anyone around Charles and I. My mom dated him for awhile before we ever met him. I was still young so most of this story comes from my mom and Charles telling me about what happen during that time. I was just in Kindergarten when he came into our lives so I don't remember much at 5 years old.

When he moved in Charles did not like it at all. Charles was the typical boy saying "he ain't my daddy so it's whatever". He gave the dude much problems and did not care if he got his ass beat. He would take whatever the punishment was and act as if it never happened. I remember one time Charles wanted to go to a party and he was disrespectful to the dude so mom said he could not go. The dude said he can go but he gone get this ass beating first by me or he can't. Charles took the beating and didn't even cry but he went to the party. He didn't care he didn't like the dude and he made it clear in his actions. Now me on the other hand I saw what Charles was getting and I did not want it so I learned to respect him but that was it. I wanted my dad not him but I had some since lol. I didn't want any parts of the beating I saw Charles get so I played it cool. I knew he made my mom happy. The dude did things for her no

other man did. He took her on trips to Jamaica &
Hawaii. He made her smile, laugh and feel
safe. He bought her cars. She did not have to work but
mom was super independent so she had to make
money for herself. She told me it felt good for a man to
take care of ALL THE BILLS for a chance. He made it
to where she could do the things she did for us. He
really took care of her and she loved him for that so I
did it for her because Charles gave her enough
problems and she told me I would respect him or else.
So I did not have a choice plus I did not want the
craziness from my mom lol.

I was the good child. I was too scared to do stuff.
Anyway our lives was pretty good until mom became ill.
She started getting dizzy spells and real bad
headaches. She worked so much she thought it was
just her being tired. She decided to go see the doctor
and found out she had brain tumors. I was still young
so I really did not understand how serious it was. I was
kept in the dark. My mom had to have biopsy done right
away. The tumors were benign which means non
cancerous but they still had to be removed because
they could turn dangerous if they press on your blood
vessels or nervous system. They cut her open from the

top of her brain to behind her ear. Technology was not as advanced as it is now so it left a very bad scar. It took them about 3 hours to remove the tumors but she made it through.

I remember coming to the hospital to see my mom. I was told I ran away when I saw her because She was so swollen and seeing those staples in her head scared me so I could not be in her presents. I was still young so I could not understand what was going on with her. They kept me away until she came home. I talked to her on the phone most of the time.

Now when I say my mom is a strong women I mean just that. She came home and got to work. She started physical therapy but it was very hard sometimes. She had to learn how to walk, talk, write simple sentences and even type so she could go back to her job. When the physical therapist was not there James, Charles and even little old me had to help mom around the house, cooking, cleaning etc.

After about 3 months mom was back at it again. She was working her job as if she never left it. They gave my mom a welcome back party. She was so surprised and thankful that she was missed and valued as an employee. The dude stayed with her through it all so I kinda had a little more respect for him after this happened to my mom. They was not married so he could have left but he didn't so I tried to be nicer.

Me, mom and the dude would sit in the bed and play cards. He loved to play tunk. I use to watch him and mom play with quarters or dollars. They eventually taught me and then I was gambling lol. How sad is that but I would beat them a lot of the time walking away with $40 dollars cuz he did not like to lose so he would say I got more money so come on let's keep playing. I learned a valuable lesson stop while your ahead because one night I had $60 and ended up with $20 lol.

It seemed to be a pretty good life again. Mom was happy so that's all that matters until mom and The dude started to argue a lot. I noticed he would come in all times of the night and because my room was next to there's I heard a lot of what was going on. It was clear The dude was cheating. I felt
It was my job to protect my mom so I started snooping around to see if I could catch him and eventually I did. I remember going to my mom and telling her about what

I saw and before I could tell her the rest she slapped me in my face and told me to stay out of grown folks business. I learned a valuable lesson that day. If you see someone cheating stay the fuck out of it and until this day that has not changed. She still stayed with him and from then on the dynamics of our relationship changed. I actually lost respect for my mom.

Honestly mom and I had a different type of mother daughter relationship. I knew she loved me but she did not say it much. She showed her love and I was ok with it. She would say she loved me if I said I loved her first. I believe my mom was that way because of her up bringing on the farm. They just worked hard all the time and rarely had time for fun. I don't really know it's just me guessing. I really never asked her about it. We did do things together like getting up on Saturday's and going garage and estate sale shopping. We found some of the best stuff at those homes. Mom loved antiques and she loved to buy chairs and redo them. She also liked to get stuff off the street that someone threw away. What someone thought was trash she thought they was crazy for throwing it away.

I still go out shopping when I can with my daughters just like mom and I did. The best place to go are is off Preston road. We would also go into Plano. Mom did not do freeways but she new the back streets. We would leave around 7am and get back around 2p. The earlier the better or you would miss out. Sometimes we would leave around 6:30a just so we could get out there fast. She drove so damn slow that's why it took so long lol. Those were the days. We would stop at some of those million dollar houses and find stuff for the low low. Some of it was new and some stuff was gently used. That's why thrifting ain't new that's just garage and Estate sale shopping lol.

Mom worked a lot during the week so when the weekend hit that was our together time. That was the time we was on the same page and we could just talk and shop for hours. The one thing that bothered me was she didn't make it easy to talk to her about things that was important like boys, kissing & sex. Whenever I tried she would always say Monica keep your legs closed. All boys want is your goodies and if you kiss them you gone get pregnant . Y'all my momma was dead ass wrong for telling me that shit but I believed it. She was my mom so what was I supposed to do. I remembered I kissed this boy in middle school and thought I was pregnant. I never told my mom but I found out I wasn't pregnant after an entire year lol. I told my brother and he said girl that's not how you get pregnant. I swear I thought kissing would get me pregnant until I started high school no lie. A boy could not touch it, smell it, kiss me and if you wanted a hug. I would stick my butt out. Y'all it was bad. I was so GREEN. I was the scary one.

It was just her way of making sure I didn't make her a grandmother before my time and it worked. When I started high school I wanted to hang more with my friends but my mom would not let me. She kept a tight rope around me neck. She even put me on birth control because she thought I was having sex and I wasn't. It was crazy how she did me sometimes but funny now that I think of it. The only free time I got was when I played sports and did cheerleading. I had cheerleading practice before school and then I had volleyball after school. I also loved game days so that meant I came home late. This was my get away that made me happy. I was the strongest right side attacker on the team. I was also the captain. I was cold. I was all district my senior year. That means I was the coldest volleyball player in my district. It had to be voted on by coaches and referees so yeas I was the chic. I always wanted my mom to be at my games but she could never come because of work. I would get mad when I saw other mothers at the games. I was a star player and did not have my mom there in the flesh to see me in action. It hurt me so bad for many year. I would alway hear her say momma wishes she could be there but I gotta work. I know she saw the disappointment in my face but she had work.

As a freshmen in high school it was an entire new world. It was where I found myself and really started to like boys more. I wasn't little Monica no more I was Monique aka Mo. I remember when we had a talent show and my brother Charles talked me into doing it. I was scared then a motherfucker y'all. I only sang at my church. I knew those people but it would be everybody from the school in the auditorium and 9th-12th grade would be there. Nobody really knew I could sing. They knew I was a bad ass at sports but not singing . I remembered that day like it was yesterday. My brother told me to sing Sweet Love by Anita Baker. It's was one of my favorite songs as well as his. He dressed me up in a sweater skirt, black lace top, some pumps and read lace gloves. People was getting Boo'd off the stage so I was scared as as hell. They introduced me to the stage and people was like Mo you better know how to sing or we gone dog yo ass lol. I said, I can watch me. So the music came on and I stared to sing and you should have see the crowd. They was like she can sing lol. I was getting into it they was cheering and the damn mic broke. It fell apart for some reason. I was about to cry and my brother stood up and stared clapping. He said, finish the song Mo you got it. I stared back singing and they bought me another mic. I had the best time that day. I was just a girl who knew how to play sports but then I was known for singing. I was in many talent shows after that. I did EnVogue with 3 other ladies and we tore it up. Man those where the times. I miss those days. I knew I was having the time of my life just growing and learning who I was as a young lady. Clowning in school, running with the popular crowds and making good grades. All the way up to my senior year. It was August of 1990 when it all started. In my head I'm about to be grown. My mom couldn't tell me what to do any more all the typical bullshit we as teenagers think we know. It was supposed to be the time of my life until something happened that changed my world forever.

Something was wrong with my mom again. She was always good at keeping stuff from me. She never wanted me to worry about her so she would always put on her mask that everything was ok even if it wasn't. I rarely saw my mother cry or show signs of weakness. In my eyes she was a superwomen.

I started to notice her continued headache. She was stubbing all over the place. She had blackouts. She was more tired than usuals. I was like mom you sure you ok? I would tell her you working to much mom you need to chill. She would always say Monica I'm ok. So like the typical teenager I would go on as if all was ok. So one day when I came home from a Friday night volleyball game. Charles and mom was at the kitchen table talking. I was like what's up y'all and my mom said sit down Monica. I'm like oh boy what I do. She said nothing just listen. I went to the doctor and they ran some test. The results came back and I have another tumor in my head. I immediately got sick at the stomach. I thought this was over. What do you mean another tumor? She told us she had to have surgery soon because this tumor was bigger and it could cause nerve damage if they didn't get it out. It was also a chance that mom would not survive this surgery. She could possible die on the operating table. Hearing all of this scared the shit out of me. It's wasn't like the first surgery in 1978 when I was just 5 and didn't really know what was going on. I was a senior in high school at the prime of my life. I was on student council, Cheerleading, Captain of the Volleyball team. I mean I was doing it. I didn't want to loose my mom. It's was a struggle from then on.

So after we the discussion mom went into the hospital for the second time to remove the tumor. The surgery went on for hours but when the doctor finally came out he said we removed the tumor and she is stable but not out of the woods. We had to resuscitated Ms Roberts two times while she was under. He said this tumor was a little more aggressive to remove than the last one. She is very weak. So she needs a lot of rest and physical therapy. I wanted to see her but the doctor said not for a few days. I just cried.. I wanted my mom. I wanted to see if she was ok. Since I could not see her I went home. Charles was out of school so he stayed with me at the house. On day three I could finally see my mom and before I could get in the door the doctor told us she caught pneumonia. We had to wear mask before we could go see her. The doctor said she is a fighter but the pneumonia was getting the best of her so they are keeping her stable for now. I walked up to the bed and said hey momma how you feeling and she gave me a thumbs up. She could not talk because they had tracheostomy tube in her throat so she could breathe. I told her I loved her and she gave me a thumbs up. I couldn't stay long because she needed her rest but it also hurt to see my mom like that. She was fighting for her life and I felt helpless. All I could do is pray. I told God I needed my mom please don't take her from me not yet not now.

I had the hardest time in school for awhile. I couldn't concentrate for nothing. I was just depressed but my volleyball coach Mrs Stratford stepped in and made sure I snapped out of it. She reminded me that you think your mom would be ok with you letting your grades slip. Of not and I'm not gonna let you fail either. You are the captain of this volleyball team and it's your senior year. We will do together what your mom can't do. I loved that women and she loved my mom. My mom's friend Rona came to see about me daily. When I say it took a village mom had everybody in place to make sure I was seen about and taken care of.

Mom got sick was around prom, senior activities, baccalaureate, senior trips etc. Mrs Stratford and Rona made sure I was involved in all of it. I was so thankful for these ladies helping but I wanted my mom. I remembered prom was coming up and I didn't want to go. Rona came and picked me up and took me dress shopping . I was such a tomb boy and didn't like dresses but I wanted to shock my mom and my friends by wearing one. The dress was royal blue, it went around my neck, with a deep V in the front and my back was out. I was like that's it. I tried it on and even Rona said that's the dress. Show them legs she said lol. I got all my hair cut off into a short style. I just went all out. I had makeup on as well. I was a totally different girl.

I went up to the hospital to show mom how I looked. It was late to come because she was in ICU but they let me in to see her. I walked in the room and she was sleep. I touched her and her eyes got big lol. She asked me for the pen and paper and she wrote "Monica you cut your hair." Then she wrote you look beautiful. She teared up and so did I. I wish you could have been with me. She wrote on the paper "I'm always with you

She said, Monica go have fun at prom. You only have one and I don't want you to miss it. It was hard at first but my friends made sure I had the best time. Everyone was surprised to see me but happy I was there. When I walked into the room all eyes was on me. This guy I really liked said damn Mo you look good. I loved all the attention. It was a fun night.

The next big event was the baccalaureate in the auditorium. This is when all my family was supposed to show up. We walked into the auditorium in all white. I was in a dress again so you know everybody was freaking out that I was in a dress. After we all marched in and sat down different people got up and spoke starting with the principle, teachers and staff. I was really enjoying it until they ask for all the family and friends to stand up and acknowledge there children. I just broke down in tears and ran out. Everybody thought my mom had died but that was not the case I just wanted her there. My dad wasn't there but my brother was and he stopped me in the hall and talked to me. He said I got you Mo for momma. I hugged him and as I turned around and most of my class was standing in the hall showing me mad love. They was like family to me as well. They had my back and wanted to help me through not having mom there. I'm so thankful for them and how they rallied around me during my time of pain. I will always be grateful. Shout out to the class of 1991. Yeah I'm showing my age a little.

Well before I could get my cap and gown I had to pass the test called theTEAMS test. I was not good at test taking and math was the part of the test I was afraid of not passing. If you fail any part of that test I could not graduate with my class. I remember telling mom I was scared because I had not got the results back yet so why should I even worry about cap and gown. My mom told me you passed it Mo. Stop defeating yourself. You are smart and intelligent. She said did you do your best and I said yes then that's all that matters. I finally received the results and could not open them. You had to make a 700 or better to be able to graduate. I went to the hospital and let mom open it. She said you passed. Y'all I made a 700 on the dot in math. I'm like they lord Hurd my humble cry. I was screaming so loud in the hospital that the nurses and doctors ran in the room thinking something was wrong with my mom. Damn fools she still can't talk so why would they think it was her screaming. She had a trake in her neck remember. We just looked at each other and laughed. It was good to see her smile. I was glad the worst was over. The doctor said she will fully recover but she will have some scaring and her speech will be slurred because during the operation some of her vocal cords got damaged. I was fine with hearing that. I was just glad once again my mom beat the odds for the second time. I tell ya she is the strongest women I know. She has always been a fighter. I just thanked God for not talking her away from me. I needed her and God new it that's why he spared her life in my eyes.

The next day we had cap and gown day at school next stop I'm officially out of school. I remember taking my cap and gown up to the hospital to show mom. I walked in the room and she was standing by the bed with a walker. She had finally started physical therapy so she was looking better. She wanted to surprise and boy was I surprised. Look at you mom standing up. I hugged her and she sat back down on the bed. She wrote on the paper I'm proud of you Monica. I know it's been hard for you but you made me proud by not giving up and not graduating. She told me she was scared for me but she also knew she raised me to start what I finish and that she wouldn't always be around so I needed to carry on and be the best me I could. She said thank you and I love you. Man if I didn't cry like a new born baby lol. Those words forever stayed with me.

Graduation day was near. I was so ready to finally be out of school. I went to the hospital hugged mom and said I'm off the graduation. My brother was there and a few other family members who stood in the gap for my mom. When they called my name to get my diploma everybody was screaming my name it was so cool. I felt like a celebrity. I was so happy but sad because mom couldn't be there but she was there is spirit. I threw my hat up in the air and it was over. Now it was time for a new chapter the grown one.

Mom came home from the hospital but she still has to once again learn how to walk, talk, write etc again with physical therapy. I was there to help her along the way. I had a scholarship for Volleyball to Jarvis Christian college but turned it down because I wanted to be with my mom. The fact I did not know if she would live or die was the reason I stayed in Dallas to attend Cedar Valley community college. My mom wanted me to go off but she allowed me to make my own decision. So I stayed and till this day I don't feel bad at all at staying by her side. I got a job at Target and went to community college. My mom always told me try college and if it's not for you then you have to figure out what you want to do. I play volleyball in college as well and was best all around in DCCD again ya girl was cold. My mom finally got a change to come see me play and I was in my prime until a girl from the opposite team had her foot under the net. I am came down on it and almost snapped my ankle. I was so hurt but it was funny watching my mom come across that court to see about her baby girl. I felt like a little kid lol. I didn't have much of the college. I went to some parties but I just worked and went to school. I also went to UTA for a year but just found out it wasn't for me. I started to work temp jobs and get certified in Microsoft office, excel, PowerPoint so I could build a resume. I really did not like working at Target to much so I wanted to leave it but not before I found another job. One of my old school buddies came through one night at work. It was cool to see her. We kicked it outside my job a few times and all was good until my ass let her talk me into some shit. I was skip scanning stuff for her and me at my job. Then I let her talk me into using stolen credit card numbers. She would come through my line with a credit card number and I would manually type it in. Sometimes cards would not scan so that's how we did it. All was good until I she used a card with my name on it and put a credit card number on the back of it. I did not know they had been watching cashiers. They caught her at the door took her upstairs and she blamed it all on me and she had my card so they believed her. They let her go cuz they wanted me. I was so embarrassed when they got me upstairs. I was handcuffed and taken to jail. Yes ya girl was a jail bird. Man I was scared as hell but I had to call my mom. When she heard there was a collect call from Lew Sterrett will you accept the changes she thought it was Charles. I said, "mom it's Monica". She said, "I know this shit is a joke". Monica, what the fuck did you do. Mom don't cuss but she cussed me the fuck out and then said I'm gone leave yo ass down there and hung up. I wasn't going to cry not in jail but I was hurt. I hurt my mom and I embarrass myself. I was in the holding cell with a girl who had speeding tickets, one was shop lifting, prostitute, a women who stabbed her husband and me at credit card fraud lol. I did not eat, sleep nothing and I sat in a corner where I could see all these women. My cuz got me out of jail the next day. He took me home and it was bad. My mom would not talk to me all. It took us a month to speak to each other again but we got through it. I had to serve 2 years deferred adjudication and it would be taken off my record. I went to work and back home for those 2 years. I didn't do shit. Once it was up I still continued my schedule. I started to get into music. I met this girl online from Houston, TX. I started working with her on a song she wrote. I would end up in Houston at least once a month. It was my first time in a studio and I loved it. One weekend I was down in Houston and I got a call from my mom and I heard sirens and police in the back ground. My mom said Monica, the house is on fire. I was like what you mean then my neighbor got on the phone because my mom was very upset. She left the house and forgot to turn and stove off because she was boiling some water for her coffee. I came home the next day to see everything I owned was destroyed.

All I had was what was in my gym bag but it was ok because my my mom was ok and that's all that matters. She had insurance so the house would be rebuilt. We stayed in a hotel for a little while and then with my aunt Carrie and then with my brother and his wife. It was a lot but we made it through. We was still standing. It did not break us.

2

The Queens Courtship

His name was Tyrone Moore He was a 6'0 tall light skinned mixed brother with light green eyes. I met him in the parking lot of Park Avenue. This was a jumping spot in the late 90's. I was with one of my girls. It was a Saturday night and we was out parking lot pimping before we went into the club. That's when you are looking for the fine ass dudes who was hanging in the parking lot. I had this new 1996 Black Volkswagen Jetta. I always kept a nice ride. I was single no kids and ready to have some fun. We was circling the parking lot and I saw him in a red and black checkered shirt with some khaki pants with some dress shoes. He just looked up at me and stared at me. I was like damn umm open your mouth and say something and he signaled for me to come over. He was with one of his homes boys on the passenger side of the car. I stopped and he said Hello my name is Tyrone what's yours I said Keshia.. Yes I gave fake names back in the day. I don't care how good you look I don't know you like that so that's what I did until I thought it was safe to tell you my real name. We talked for a minute and exchanged numbers. He called me immediately the next day. I was like damn he must really want to get to know me. He asked could he come see me and I said, NO! I don't invite people to my home I just met sorry. He said, well you can come to my place. I said umm NO! What part of I don't know you don't you understand. I don't know you or trust you at this point. We can meet at a public place or we won't meet at all. He said ok my bad. I was about to hang up on his ass because I don't like pushy dudes.

He stayed in North Dallas so I came out that way and we met at some little food place by the North Park mall. Things have changed in that area so I can't remember the name just the area. I've always been a little straight forward when talking to dudes. I just let them know I'm not about them games, what do you really want, you got any kids, babymomma drama, what you do for a living, you got your own place. Yes just call me private investigator. He actually laughed and said ok I'm from Madison Wisconsin but I was raised in Ore City, Tx.. It's a little town not too far from Longview Tx. I have no kids, I have a warehouse job I just started working, I have my own apartment and I have a car. I was like jackpot because most of the dudes I was meeting did not have shit. They just wanted some ass and try and move in with you. Hell to the Naw Naw and Naw. I was so tired of that. If you had potential I was willing to work with you but you had to have something of your own. Then he said, what about you. I was like you ready lol. He said yeah since you asking me all these questions. Well, I live with my mom, I've been on my job for 6 years, I don't have no kids & I have my own car. He asked why don't you have your own place (eyebrow raised) well I was going to move with a homegirl of mine but she had some habits I was not cool with so I knew living with her would be a disaster. I was going to move by myself but my mom said whats the rush you don't have to move so soon. Even if I did move I would always end up at my moms house after work because she was always cooking lol. She would call and ask me what you want to eat. I would honestly chill with my mom. It would get late and I'd either fall asleep or go home to my place but most of the time it would be me sleeping at my moms house. I knew my mom didn't want me to leave so it just worked out. I paid half the bills so I was ok with living with her. I also did not have a man in my life worth moving in with so I was ok with arrangement. He was like ok I understand. We talked about a lot of things and he was pretty cool. I had to eventually tell him my real name. He actually did not get mad he said you don't look like a Keshia, I'm like what does that mean. He said most Keshia's are ghetto. I'm like see that's what's wrong with people stereo typing but ok you got your opinion.

We went out on a few more dates continuing to get to know each other. It was kinda like we gradually started to be in a relationship without saying we was. Y'all know that's a problem when it comes to relationships. You have not said I want to be in a relationship but you acting as if you are. Well I actually said what we doing. He said what you mean. It's been like 2 months are we in a relationship or what he said yes we are. I was like you ain't asked me shit. You just assuming I'm yo girl. I think not. He just laughed and said Mo will you be my women. My smart as was like I don't know it took you to long. He was like come on now. I was just messing with him. I said ok, let's give it a try.

Now during this time he still had not met my mom or my brother lol. I don't play y'all. If you wasn't something I wanted to bring home to my family I would keep you hidden. I live by that rule. I don't need you meeting them then you gone weeks later then I'm looking like a fool in front of my family. I needed to know you was gone be around. During all this time I never went to his place and he never went to mine. I wanted us to get to know each other without sex being involved. So I finally went to his place. It was a nice apartment and that's all that mattered but shortly I found out he had guest. His Cuzzin, Cuzzin wife and their children living with him. He explained that they needed a place to stay and he was helping them out. He said they was only gone be there for a few months but that turned into more than a few months but it was his family so I didn't say much. I remember meeting his brother one night when we went out. He took me to some party and introduce me to him. Y'all I was dead ass wrong but his brother looked better than him. He was just shorter. I actually started low key flirting with him and I think Tyrone noticed it I guess. I was just sitting on the couch having a conversation with his brother. They was smoking weed and drinking. I had some drinks but I didn't smoke weed. It just wasn't my thing so I stepped outside. His brother came outside with me. We was just talking and laughing when Tyrone came outside. He told him there you go getting all up in my girls face. I assumed he had issues with his girls leaving him for his brother. I will say this if I didn't have a guilty conscience I would have dumped him and dated his brother. Yes I know Mo you trash for that comment lol. Well I'm telling the truth but I decided I didn't want to cause issues with him and his brother so I let it be. I really like Tyrone it's just that lust inside you when you see someone else that looks good and you think the grass is greener on that side that's all.

I finally decided to let him meet my mom after about 6 months of dating. My mom knew something was up but she never really said anything. She always waited on me. I told her I'm going to introduce you to Tyrone. I've been dating him for months now. It's kinda serious so she said ok bring him over. I called him and told him mom wants to meet you can you come over this weekend. He was silent for a moment and said ok cool. I said I thought you would be happy to meet my mom and she said I am I just never thought it would happen. I just laughed and said well it's happening. He came over and was scared. He didn't know what to say to mom so she just told him you better be good to my daughter. I know you will have your problems but don't you ever put your hands on her or you will answer to me and some other family. He just said yes ma'am. She said now that we have and understanding let's eat hahahaha my mom straight crazy. Where you think I get it from. We straight to the point. My momma and Ty developed a pretty good relationship and that made me happy. He also got a chance to meet my brother Charles. Charles was cool with him but low key did not like him. He didn't like to much of any dude I dated but he was normally on point when he felt they was not the one. Charles said, if my sister love you I love you but keep yo hands to yourself man or you gone have some problems when it comes to me. I think he understood keep your hands to yourself or you gone be dead. They develop a pretty good bond as well so my side was ok with him.

He said now since I met your family I feel it's time to meet mine. We had to take a trip to Ore City, to meet his family. It took about 2 1/2 hours to get there. I swear when we got there you could blink and then you was out of that little town hahah. We went to go see his dad first. Elisha aka Bimbo. I did not have to meet with a mother because him and his mom was estranged. He didn't know her but he knew of her. She left his dad when he was a baby. Kinda like my story but his was more like his mom left because they family did not agree with mixed children so I was told. When we got there we pulled up to a trailer home and before we could get out of the car we was greeted by Grandma, this women was like a mother to Ty. He would always talk about her and I would hear him talking on the phone to her. She said "so you are Monique huh". Well nice to meet you. He been running his damn mouth about you for months now. I just laughed cause Ty said "Grandma don't embarrass me. She said boy shut you ass up. Hey every other word was a cuss word coming out this women's mouth. She was real and raw. She turned around and yelled Bemmm short for Bimbo Tyrone is here with that girl Monique. When his dad came out I was like yep that's your dad only a darker version with light brown eyes. He spoke to me and told Tyrone you did a good job with this one. I'm like this one. She's cute. I just laughed it off but my eyebrows raised. What the hell he mean this one. Well we went inside Grandma Trailer and I felt like I was in Ozan, AR again with my Madea. No running water or heat We had to go down to his aunt Fannie house to bathe. I swear I did not like that at all but it's all good cuz I've lived like that before but I did not want to make to many trips down there if that's how it was gonna be. I had graduated from that way of living.

We went to visit some other family. We ended up buying something to drink and chill under this tree at grandma house. It wasn't much to do down there honestly but drink and that was not my thing. We went home the next day and I told my mom how it was and she said Monica give it a chance. I told her I would because I loved him and so I did. We continued to date and all was going well. This was the longest relationship I had been in for awhile so I was pretty happy. One night we was having dinner and he said "Mo will you marry me"and I said, No! He said "why"and I said you not ready for marriage. He said I'm going to show you I am. You see I'm older than Ty by 5 years so I felt we was in a good place and didn't need to be married. I just enjoyed dating. He tried it again and I said No again. So one night we went bowling with some friends and family and he said he had a surprise for me. Why this boy get down on one knee and asked in-front of his family to marry me and I actually broke down and said yes. I did not know he had already talked to my mom and she was ok with it.

My brother found out and he said I don't think he's the one but if that's what you want I'll respect that. My brother the protective one. I love him. He has always had my back. Not too long after I said I will the wedding plans started to take place. I felt that since I was getting married that we needed our own place for the the first time ever we went apartment shopping. I was excited but sad because I was moving away from mom and starting a new life. We found an apartment in North Dallas. It was a one bedroom apartment and it was nice. My mom as always helped me make it a home. We moved in like a month before our wedding. I swear I was scared but I knew it was time to be on my own. It was different coming home to my own place instead of moms house but it was worth it.

After getting settled in the apartment I decided to go with a wedding planner because I was not good at picking out stuff. I know she would help guide me and pick my brain on how I wanted it to be. To be honest I really did not care. I was not a girlie girl. I was not super picky. If she showed me something I normally would say that's cool. She said I was the easiest client she ever had in years. I went with Teal and burgundy for my colors. It just looked good. I had all my brides maidens dresses hand made. I had a heart shaped arch and we where married in a church down the street from my moms house. My wedding dress came from Terry Costa. It was gorgeous and only $250. I did not feel I needed a dress that cost thousands of dollars. My mom went out of her way to make sure this wedding was unforgeable. I felt like a princess. The day of my wedding was simply extraordinary. To see it was better than imagining it. I was so happy. My dad actually showed up but I let my brother gave me away. He had been with me all my life. It was only fare to him. We said our vowels and I was married. The new Chapter begins.

Tyrone wanted to get started having a child as soon as possible. I was like nope we just got married lets take our time. We need to enjoy each other. He was mad about it for awhile so I went and talked to mom about it. She told me that if I wasn't ready then don't do it. A baby is a big responsibility that means no more just about Monica. It will be about the baby first. I understood this and just wanted to wait. I was not sure if I was ready to give up doing me when I wanted to but it's not just about me anymore it's about Ty and I so we started the process. It took me at least a year to get pregnant. I had been taking birth control pills for years so my doctor said it will take some time. One night Ty and I was out having some fun and we had an argument because this dude tried to talk to me in the club. I just wanted to go home because it didn't have to get out of hand like it did. Ty had been drinking and his stupid came out so I said let's go. We argued most of the way till I told him take me to my moms house. We was coming across the MLK bridge and he was driving fast and crazy. I said "you need to claim down". The last thing I remember was him saying 'if I can't have you know body can. He tried to get between two cars and lost control of the car hitting the bridge head on. I don't remember much except waking up in the street laying on this ladies chest and her telling me to hold on help is on the way.

I got to the hospital still kind of out of it. When they got me in the room they lifted me on this table and a bunch of ER people was cutting off clothing because I had a gash on my knee, large bump on my head and both my hands where swollen because when the airbag deployed I put my hands up to cover my face.

I remember this nurse asking me are you pregnant and I said, "not that I know of." She told me we need to do X-rays on your head so we need to make sure your not pregnant. She said, "I'm going to need a urine sample."I had to lay still strapped down while she put a damn pan under my ass. It was the most embarrassing shit of my life. While they was waiting on the results the other nurse came in and cleaned my wound and all the blood from the gash on my leg. They gave me some numbing medicine and then stitched it up. The ER doctor came back in and said well we can't do any X-rays on your because your pregnant. I was like what you mean pregnant. He said congratulations and you will be ok. All your vital signs are stable you'll just be sore for awhile. I just started crying. Not because I was pregnant but because I didn't know I was and could have lost this baby but God had a plan so I was thankful that little life survived. I just wanted to see my mom. My brother's wife was walking by and heard the doctor say I was pregnant and she ran in the room jumping up and down. Then my mom can in. I was scared to tell her. I was 25 years old and scared to tell my mom I was pregnant. She asked, you ok? I said yes besides my head, hands and knee hurting I'm good. I said well I'm pregnant and she said ok. Is the baby alright? I said as far as I know it is. Well then ok. I was like she was cool with me being pregnant. I'm all scared like she was about to whoop my ass or something. Well after they released me I went home to my moms house. I did not want to see Tyrone at all. His behavior almost got us killed. It made me question if I still wanted to be with him. He called I would not answer. This went on for a few days until he showed up. My mom let him in and I was kinda mad at her but she said that's enough. You gotta talk to him. He came in apologizing and said it was the alcohol and he would never do it again. Please don't leave me Mo. They fact that I was carrying his baby honestly was the only reason I stayed. I told him I was pregnant and he broke die crying. He seemed remorseful so I forgave him.

We went home and all was good for the meantime. He was a very loving man. He saw about me all the time and wanted to make sure I was ok. I worked my entire pregnancy and it was hard. Feet swelling, falling asleep at the computer, & not wanting to get up. All the stuff that comes with pregnancy but I did it. My job at the time gave me a beautiful baby shower and I had another shower at my moms house. I receive a lot of great gifts from everybody. My job made me go on leave because my intentions was to work until I went into labor and they was not having it so a week before my due date they sent me on leave. It's was good they did because I went into labor that Tuesday and had my baby girl Tyler Wednesday mornings. I remember laying on the table getting prepared for the c-section and they let Tyrone come in to be by my side. I cried he cried it was such a beautiful moment in our lives our very first child together. Life was so good. I stayed in the hospital for 5 days and we finally went home. We had moved from the apartment into a rent house down the street from my mom. I just wanted to be closer to her and I did not like apartments and she could help me when needed.

Man let me tell you being a mom for the first time grew my ass up even at 26 years old. That every 2 hour feeding and pamper changing can wear you down but Tyler was a good baby. She normally cried when she was hungry and wanted to be changed otherwise she was good. I also could not stand being in the house for 6 damn weeks. It felt like prison. Ty would help but not as much as I would want a husband to help. He said, I'm tired. I slapped him upside that head and said so am I. You better help me or there will be problems. He was off an entire week for his leave. But it didn't matter because I knew I would be doing all the work. Tyler started growing like a weed. I was having so much fun with her. She had such personality. We went to the 1st doctor visit and she was healthy and growing the way she should. Her jaundice had went completely away and I was so happy because it could have killed her. She's a fighter.

Once I went back home my mom told me she was gonna help me but I did not want to bother her. She said girl that's my grand baby. I'm going to help you because you need it. I had my normal routine down with her help. Take Tyler to the daycare, go to work, pick her up and go home. Sometimes she would go get her from the daycare so I could just come home. I really appreciate her because Ty was really not helping me much. He started checking out on our relationship. He was complaining about how hard it was. He truly expressed he was not happy. Ty and I argued a lot because he started staying out late and drinking more than usual. He always had somebody at the house or fighting dogs in the garage. He would go down to visit his family more than usual. It was always some shit with him. I swear I felt like he was cheating but I had no proof. His behavior changed and so did his patterns. I was catching him in lies. It was bad but I wanted my married to work so I put up with some shit I shouldn't have to be honest but I didn't want to be another statistic. A baby mom with a child and no husband. This shit went on for many years. His family started to stay with us on and off. It seemed like we never had privacy. It was like they never had a secure place to live. They was living with each other or living off someone. It was not a life style I was use to but I never said no so it was some of my fault as well. He started loosing jobs because he was so drunk he couldn't get up to go to work. The weight of the house was on my shoulder. I was always the #1 bread winner and he never had a problem with it but he began to get lazy. We needed another car and so my mom helped me get a little cash car for him to get back and forth to work. He was not looking for a job so I help him find one. He finally got the job at DHL and that made me happy because I needed help. He started to do better but the drinking increased more and we fought more. I would leave Tyler over my moms because I did not like her seeing what was happening. His dad moved in with us for awhile and that's when more shit started. I came home one day from being over my moms house until about 8p. I walked in and saw all these mother fuckers in my house. He thought it was ok to have his homeboys over with they side chicks. I was not having that shit at my house. I made one bitch jump the balcony because I told them whores you not walking back through this house without getting your ass beat. I cussed his ass out and a few of his boys I knew had girls at home.

Don't bring that shit to my house. Then yo bitches looking at me thinking I was ok with this shit. Then I went in on Ty ass. I said, "so this the shit you do." I said, you got a bitch as well I'm sure". It's was ugly. He slept in his car that Damn night. He also thought it was ok to come home the next day while parting with his dad. I was on my way to work that day and I locked the inside lock. He was locked out all night. When he knocked on the door I greeted his ass and slapped the fuck out of him. The shit I put up with y'all. I should have bounced but again I didn't. I stayed for Tyler and wanting to save my marriage. I loved him (I was a fucking fool).

We continue to try and work things out but time and time again I would get the same results. I got so tired of always seeing someone at our house. We was never by ourselves man. That's shit got irritating. Always drinking, smoking and bullshitting. During that time the song I think you better call Tyrone came out and I swear it was the truth. Every time you come around your gotta bring Jim, James Paul and Tyrone. I was really getting tired.
The last straw was when he lost the job at DHL. I was pissed. I just got tired of being in the same predicament. There was minimal change or effort on his part. It was time to talk about separation or something but before I could He started applying for his unemployment and got a par-time job at Arby's. Once again I was like well he trying

so I didn't say anything. I just wanted to see what he would do. It was timed out on telling me. You gotta show me. He was doing good until he fell back into his old habits. Slowly he started hanging out more and more. He never stopped drinking but he began to drink heavier. He then started to hanging with my Cuzzin Jamie. The only way I found out is he called me and said, "Mo I saw yo hubby last night." I said wear? He said at this spot I be hanging out at. He said, "It's cool cuz". He ain't doing nothing wrong just shooting pool, talking shit, drinking and stuff. I was like ok cool but I still did not like it.

Anyway one day one of my friends names Angela called me and said ummm I don't want to cause no problems but I love you and I don't want to see you hurt. I was like Awww shit what is it. She said I saw your husband, outside with this girl all hugged up outside of Arby's. I called his name and he acted like he did not see me so I called his name again. Then he and the girl walked inside the restaurant. I was like ok and thank you. I'm not mad at you at all. I was not going to confront him yet. I'm the type who let you get real comfortable and then I come for yo ass where you can't even fix your damn lips to lie. I was also crazy to think maybe he was just talking to a coworker and it was too loud for him to hear her. Ladies you know we rationalize about what we see or what we where told. Then I snapped out of it. The things we put ourselves through.

But anyway his behavior continued and it got worse so again my Cuz called me and said hey I need to talk to you and I'm like ok cool. I met up wit him and his girl at the time. When I saw him I knew something was up. He said, "cuz I love you and I had to tell you that I hooked up with yo husband so we could smoke a little something and he shows up wit this girl. I swear I turned all kinds of red when he said, "showed up with this girl." WTF you mean girl. He said, before you think I was cool with it I wasn't. I just wanted to see if this nigga really thought I would be ok with him bringing this bitch in front of me like I was ok with it. He said they was all hugged up sharing smoke and kissing. I swear I was in disbelief y'all. In your gut you don't want to believe that shit but I had no choice but too. He would not lie to me. Even his girl said I told him he needed to tell you. I was so hurt I couldn't think. I just told him thanks.. He said, cuz you ok. I said, naw but I will be.

In my mind I just wanted to go home and wait for him to get home and cuss his ass out but for what. I just had to be real and tell him what I knew. This shit made me doubt every getting married to him and giving him another chance. I waited until he got home. I actually had calm down and for good reason. I said husband, I need to talk to you and I'm gone tell you out the gate don't lie. He said, I don't have time for this Mo. Y'all I turned all kinds of colors. Mother fucker I tried to come to yo ass without the drama but since you wanna be a bitch about it then let's go. How about I know you cheating on me bitch. He said, what the fuck you talking about. Like almost all dudes I done dealt with say that shit. The bitch at your job nigga don't play dumb. The bitch you was all hugged up with when you was hanging out with my cuz nigga. His eyes got bigger. I ain't been with nobody. I said ok I'm leaving and he was like why. I said, "if I have to tell you why then it's over" I packed my shit and went to my moms house. Hey just lied with a straight face and that was too much for me to handle.

He was not allowed at moms house because I told her I did not want to see him. He called and even tried to come to my job and I stoped that shit. I was just tired but when I was finally ready to talk I told him unless you gone tell the truth we have nothing to talk and he stuck to the lie. I said ok, let's do some counseling. He agreed to it. The day of the council I was feeling like I was finally going to get some answers but I was dead ass wrong. He said, I don't want some stranger in our business we can work this out on our own and just walked out the session. I continued to go alone for months and I finally understood that he did not want this marriage enough to just say he cheated and how can we fix this. I just wanted to know what made him feel like he had to go out and cheat on me. I'm not perfect but I was a damn good provider and wife in my opinion.

His ass got upgraded when he got with me and he knew it. It was at that moment I knew what I needed to do. He told me once before he did not believe in divorce and he was not paying for no divorce. Y'all I took a check and a half and paid a lawyer to start the process. I was done. He tried to avoid me because I told him I filed for divorce. I had to go to his job and tell him if you don't sign the papers she will serve you the papers at your job. He said, so this how it's gonna be. I said yes it is. He said, can I come to see Tyler and I will sign them then. I agreed.

He came over late as usual drunk and shit but I told mom to let him in. He said, can we talk? I said, about what? He said come on Mo please. I said what do you want to say. Y'all what came out of his mouth made me so mad I almost punched him in the face. He said, Mo I did cheat on you and I'm sorry. I honesty don't know why I did it. It was wrong and I hope you can forgive me. I really did not think you would have divorced me. In my head I'm thinking well thats really arrogant of you mother fucker. Well you are too late. I just need you to sign the paper. The girl stayed across the street from my daughters elementary school. She worked with him on the job. She had been calling my phone talking shit and to top it off she was 19. I was just done. He signed the paper and left. I had cried all I could y'all. I had prayed all I could. I did want him anymore. He had took me through too much in 9 years and the fact that he only apologize because he saw divorce papers did it for me. It was the end. He stalked me for a while after the divorce. I remember one time catching him sleeping on Tyler's trampoline at one point. But shortly after he got the point and stopped that as well. I was sad, hurt and broken but never beaten! Even in that whole marriage I still came out strong.

3

Can't Stop the Heat

After my married was over I was done with being somebodies wife. For awhile all I did was go to work, work out at the gym and play in volleyball and softball leagues. I did not want any association with a man period. I didn't even want sex. It was serious. I manage to turn my feeling completely off. I was just tired of getting hurt and I also had to see what I was doing to allow this to happen over and over again. It's not just them all the time we got issues as well.

While I was separated from my ex I manage to meet a guy on Myspace. Y'all, I was on Black Planet, TAGGED and lord knows what other social media I was on. It was thing to do so I did it because my homegirl told me to make a profile even though I was not dating anyone. That shit was a set up. I should have never did it in my Trey Songz voice. I was trying to stay away from men but she told me it would be good for me. People started to friend you & inbox you. It was crazy. It was an easy way to get to know people without meeting face to face. But anyway, he inboxed me asked for my number and we talked on the phone. I told him I was married but separated and there was no chance of us getting back together. He said, it's cool I'm not judging. I just want have some fun and kick it. I was like ok as long as you understand I'm good. I was older than him so I knew what was up. Once again I was 5 years older than him. I need to leave 5 alone lol. Anyway he was 6'1, slender build, dark skinned. He was fine. He had a build like my ex husband. It kinda pissed me off a little but I can't get mad at him for having features I like in a man. We all have a type and I manage to get a guy built like my ex husband. We will call him dread head.

After about a few weeks of talking we decided to meet up. I called my friend to go with me. She was like, you finally going out. Hell, yeah I'm going with you. We went to this place in Lower Greenville. I can't remember the name but it was always jumping.. We didn't even get in the club good and dudes was asking can I buy you a drink. It took me a minute to adjust to not being married lol. I was like ummm sure. I said to myself he buying me a drink. Yeah buddy I'm gone take it. I was just holding conversation with this guy when Dread head walked up behind me and whispered you cheating on me already. I was about to get an attitude until he pulled me away from the other dude to the dance floor with drink in hand. I yelled, Thank you! We was dancing and grinding to the music all night long. It was the first time in 9 years I had a good time. I swear I drank so much liquor I barley remember leaving the club but I do. My girl found her a dude and she said you good. I was like yep. She said, I'm leaving with him. She knew him so I was ok.

So dread head said you ready to go and I was like yeah. Man I took two steps and could barley walk. I clearly had too much to drink. He asked, you need me to drive and I said yes because I can't. He said, where you wanna go. I said your place. Yep I already knew what's up. So we got to his place and he helped me in his house. He said, you sure you ok with this I don't want to take advantage of you. At first I was scared because I had never been with another man in years but I honestly didn't care. I just wanted to feel good for now. It was nice and he did a good job lol. A real good job and I'm gone leave it at that.

I woke up the next morning like what did I just do. I looked under the covers just naked. I was oh well that's how it is. I was about to get up and put my clothes on when he opened his eyes and said, "you ok"? I said, Yes I knew what was up and thank you. He just smiled. I had to get home. I'm sure my mom is worried about me. I normally come home. If she don't see me car she will freak out. I couldn't find my damn phone. As we was leaving a little dude came out of his room and said I was loud. Can y'all say embarrassed. Dread head said, man go back to your room. I asked him who house we at. He said his mother's house. I left that house before his mom could come out the room. I said dude come on your moms house. I was pissed. He apologized but I didn't want to hear it at that time. The walk of shame was bad. I found my phone at the

car door and it had a bunch of missed calls, voice
messages, texts etc. I called my home girl to let her know I
was ok and she cussed me out lol. It was cool. I called me
niece and she was mad because she stayed at my house
all night long worried about me hoping mom would not
come over. It was about 10am when we I left his house.

I actually laughed about it. I had some fun and that's all
that matters. Dread head called me and apologize again.
He said he should have told me he lived with him mom but
he was caught up in the moment and he said he wanted
me bad. Hey said, you know what it's cool I'm just glad
your mom did not wake up. I said, was I that loud he
smiled and said umm yep but my moms was on the other
side of the house so I wasn't worried but my brother well
he know how I get down. I was still embarrassed man.
Every time his little brother saw me he smiled at me. I just
smiled back. It was funny.

Well we continued to see each other and there was no
pressure. He actually wanted me to meet his mom and
sister and I agreed. It was cool and even his mom and
sister said you must be special because my son does not
bring many women to my house. I just smiled and said
thank you. I was tryin not to catch feeling for him but the
shit happed by default. He would come to my home and
stay sometimes. He met my mom and brother it was like

we was in a relationship but we wasn't. We was just having fun. He was a rapper and he had a little side job. He would introduce me to his friends as this is my girl Mo. She can sing y'all. I was already working on my cd so dread head opened up more doors for me to record and meet local artist. He actually was featured on one of my songs on my cd. We was still just kicking it. He finally got his own place and that was good. He didn't have much but it didn't matter. I began to hang with him at his place for awhile. He had a lot of friends that came in and out of his crib. We partied a lot but then things stared to change a little.

I showed up one night at his place. It was kinda crazy. People was drinking, smoking that good and then I saw that white girl on the table. I only drank y'all I was not a weed head or drug user. I asked him what is that on the table. He said it cocaine baby. Come on and try it with me. I'm like umm naw I don't want to do that. It can make you a drug addict. You need to stop doing it. He said, I'm not an addict and I do it sometimes. The sad part is I knew better but still tried it anyway. I had drug dealers and drug addicts in my family so you would think I wouldn't entertain it but I did ya'll I tried it. I was up all damn night just wired out of my mind. I did not like that feeling at all. He also got me to try X. I didn't like that either it dried my mouth out and it did not make me want to have sex lol. My ass was just dumb and trying shit I know I shouldn't have but I thank God that I never got addicted to any of it. I never wanted anymore of those drugs. Yes y'all girl could have been a crack head but by the grace of God I was saved.

I had to let this dude go. He just was not good for me. Any person who would try and get you caught up in the drugs was not for you. It was fun while it lasted but I had to let go and I was cool with it. I still went out and partied but I always found myself going back to social media. It was fun and I didn't have to worry about meeting anyone unless I wanted to. I met this other guy named Military man. After Dread head I wanted to take it slow in getting to know him. He was really a sweet guy. I told him the same thing I told dread head. He responded by saying I been down that road before and the women went back to her husband so we can be friends until your divorce was final. I could respect that. We pretty much talked when he was not deployed. He was gone for long periods of time and honestly I didn't like it but he asked me to just be open and understanding. Once the divorce was final he was more connected. He would sneak off base. I would tell him stop that because you gone get in trouble but he didn't care because he wanted to be with me and see me. I went to visit him on his base to pick him up in Oklahoma. He would come back for the weekend. He would have a phone where he would check in because he had people

Page 59

covering for him. I could tell he really wanted something solid. Whatever he did in the military he could not talk to me about it which made it hard for me. He said you just have to trust me. I knew it had to be serious when he put me on his Incase of emergency call me. He told me if some soldiers show up at your door I'm dead. That ain't some shit I want to hear but ok.

He wanted me to meet his mother and father and I agreed. They was super nice and I enjoyed talking to them. All was actually going well because he made sure he saw me as much as he could to make me feel comfortable. One time when he was away his ex girl reached out to me on my cell as I was coming home for work. The bitch was messy 100. She was talking mad shit about them always being together no matter what. She said why would he want you. You're not his type. Y'all I was just listening because she was just talking and I was taking it in. You will never have him like I do. All the typical bullshit girls who are mad he moved on will say. I did not engage her at all I just hung up the phone. Don't get it twisted I was pissed but I wanted to hear his side.

He came back home and I told him your ex bitch called my phone and his eyes got big. How did this bitch get my number? This is the type of shit I don't like Military dude. I don't bring drama to you so keep it away from me. This bitch don't know me. I'm not the one to be played with. If you still fucking her then we have a problems. He said just let me explain. I said ok talk but if it's bullshit we done. He told me they had been on and off for 5 years and she was use to him not being in a relationship with anyone. She also has a boyfriend. I said handle that shit because I don't have time for that. He told me he would. He called her immediately while I was standing there and told her it's all the way over I'm with Mo and hung up. He changed his number and everything so I was cool. Well that showed me he was serious about us so I decided to take him up on his offer. He asked for me to at least give it a try. I did but honestly we both had issues. I could not deal with him being gone. He kept thinking I was cheating and I didn't give him a reason to think that. He really was a good guy but he wasn't for me. We had to part but we remained friend.

Honestly I just needed to be by myself again. These dudes always wanting to cuff me up and stuff. I fell into the shit every time. So back to the old Mo. I enjoyed parting with no strings attached. It's was just easier.

I was at this Caribbean spot off 635 one night with my homegirl. She love foreign men. She said they pay what they weigh and they treat you nicer. They don't mind giving and spending money. She told me maybe this will work out. I said, girl I don't want no man. They make me tired with all they drama or extra shit. I just wanna a dial a dick. Come in perform and leave. She said ok maybe you can find one here. I was having a good time. My girl got these dude to buy us some rum punch. I should have left that shit alone but it was good. The music was off the chain and the dude looked good. As I was talking with the dude who bought me a drink this Jamaica dude I met with green eyes had been watching me all night but I just ignored him. He finally caught me at the bar. He said Aye pretty lady may I buy you a drink. I said, sure if you buy my girl one. That's how we got down. You gotta hook my girl up to and so he did. He said, what a pretty ting like you in dis club by yourself. I said just having fun. Oh so A so do ting set which means so that's they way it is pretty lady and I said yes. He said don't be so mean. Let me talk to you while you drink dat drink. I said ok cool. So we had conversations while my girl was dancing with his friend. Then Bennie man came on "Dem girl name Suga" and I started to dance a little. He said aye you dance with me and I was like ok cool. Them drinks started setting in so I was not so uptight. Man I swear this dude could dance. I had a hard time keeping up but I manage to get with his style lol. There culture is very sexual when it comes to dance so I just did me. He said I did a pretty good job but needed lessons hahaha oh well.

It was almost time to go and I had a little to much to drink but I could still drive. He was like let me take you home pretty lady. I was like no I'm good and I was with my girl. She drove ya home but before I left he said. You gone take my number. I said ok. I gave him mine and that was that.

He called me the next day wanting to go out on a date. He wanted to get to know me. I was like oh my God here we go. I told him - Jamaica is what we will call him. I don't want anything exclusive. He said me either. I was like good. I said, so tell em about you. He had his own apartment he shared with a friend, he had a cricket phone, no car and needed a green card. I was like omg yep he just need to be a dial a D. That's where I kept him at. He was trying his best to make me his women and I said I ain't helping you get a green card dude. You not gone play me like that. We can just keep it the way it is. You know your job.

He just laughed at me and said ok if that's what you want. Yep that's all I needed. While I kept him on the side I met a dude I use to know from school. I walked into a dealer ship ready to trade in my car for a newer car and someone called me Monique Roberts. I swear I did not want to turn around. I just prayed God let him be handsome hahahaha. I know that's bad but hey I had to be real. I turned around and I saw that big smile, bald head and light brown eyes. I said, Heyyyy because I could not remember his name but he knew mine. Hey did you buying a car. I said yep. I came in to look around. He told the dude who was trying to help me I got her. Dude looked pissed but brown eyes was one of the top sellers in the dealership.

He said, what you wanna drive I got you. I said, oh really now. He said yes I do. I test drove this car real nice ride he showed me. While we was out driving we got caught up. He asked, where was my man at? Typical question from a dude. I said, I don't have one. He just smiled. He said, you wanna know what I had the biggest crush on you in school man. I never had the courage to come and talk to you but I'm not gone miss my shot this time. I said, oh really well let's see then. He then said, can I take you out on a date? I said, sure. He was such a gentleman opening doors etc and using correct grammar lol. I thought it was sweet but I know that's how they start out. He asked me was David and Busters ok. I'm sure y'all saying really Mo but I love that place so I was ok with it. I was kinda excited because I hadn't been on a date in months. I got there and he lead me to the back where this nice bar was. I walked up and he was suited up smelling good and looking nice. I was like ok I'm impressed a little. He said, a little this my best attire. We just laughed. I sat at the bar and he asked what do you drink and I said Kettle one with cranberry. The bartender came around and said what's up eyes. I see you are back. I said he must bring all his women in here huh. The Bartender said naw, he come here after work to have a few drinks. But yeah the ladies be on my boy. He hasn't brought a women here in months. I'm like…thats game. He is private wing man lol. I was like yeah ok. Eyes just laughed at me. So Mo what's up girl. How you been? I just talked about I had been married and I had a daughter etc. He told me yeah not married but I have kids. I have 7. I said, dude you need to put that thang up. He said, you got jokes. Yes I know, I was wild back in my day. Running around fucking everything and everybody. I got caught up but I love all my children and they are taken care of. I said that's good or we would not even be talking. Anyway we talked and reminisced about a lot of stuff for hours and them drinks kept coming.

My ass got too comfortable. He said, lets try this drink called the blue or red pill. I said ok but this is the last once because I gotta drive home. He said ok, I got you don't worry. Why did I do that. I was good until that last damn drink. My ass could not drive home and I'm sure that's what he wanted. He helped me to the car and saw that I really could not drive. He said, can you just drive down the street. He said, just follow behind me. Y'all I turned that AC up so and it was cold outside but I manage to focus enough to get down to this Marriott hotel. He actually was a gentleman and did not do anything to me. We just talked for awhile but hey we both liquor up but he did say you sure because this was not my intentions and I said yeah yeah ok. He said, no really this is not how I planned my first date with my crush. I said, yes I'm sure and I swear I don't remember much because I was that faded lol. I know that's sad. But I didn't remember and I was naked so yeah. Yes whore tendency's but it happen and I didn't feel bad at all. We woke up and he asked was I ok. I said, yep just hung over. He said, you remember last night. I said after we got to the hotel it was kinda shaky but yes I know we had sex don't trip. He just exhale as if I said the magic word. Y'all I just didn't remember the act. Oh well. He said can I see you again I said sure.

We kicked it for awhile and then we kinda got serious without saying we was a couple. I enjoyed the way he treats me. He dropped me money on bills, he paid for airplane tickets, taught my daughter how to ride a bike and spent time with her. He did pretty much everything but commit to me. I was ok for awhile but then got caught up in feeling number one mistake. One day we was out to dinner and I had to ask so what is this we doing eyes. He said Mo don't do that. Don't you like it the way it is. I take care of you don't I. Eyes I like it but I want more and he said I don't know Mo. I said, who is she? He said, nobody. I said ok do you love me. He said, I care for you but that's all. He said come on Mo let's not do this. I told him, take me home eyes. We got to my house and I got out the car. He followed me up to my door and I said you not coming in. You not gone treat me like a side chick. He said come on that's not fare. I slammed the door and locked it. I forgot his ass had a key lol. He was like just listen to me and I said no get the fuck out now. Eyes grabbed my ass pushed me up against the wall and started kissing me. He said, you don't want me to leave. We as women can be weak as hell behind men. Then he stopped kissing me and said let me talk to you. That's code for let me mind fuck you some more. I said What! since I'm only good for sex and some dinner etc. he said, Mo you don't want to love me. I am not the loving type. I will treat you good and take care of you but love I can't do. I said, ok and I started kissing him and I said you sure about that because you always with me at my house spending the night and you work 7 days a week. I was in that mode so I was gone get what I wanted. He said, you can't love me. I swear I wish I would have listened but naw like a lot of women we fill we can change them. I continued this fucked up shit with him for awhile but I loved him and that's what made it hard to let go and he was not trying to let go of me.

This went on for awhile until. I missed my period and I thought I was pregnant. I actually was kinda happy but when I told him he said, I didn't ask for this Mo. I don't want anymore child. I said, Mother Fucker that ain't what you said when you was up in this shit yelling and screaming. When you said I do love you and all that other shit. I was hurt but it taught me some shit and I was so glad when I found out I wasn't pregnant. Don't let nobody make you feel like it's your damn fault alone and stop fucking this nigga without a condom. But my ass was still dumb. Love can fuck you up.

One day a bitch inboxed me on FB. She said, he loves me to so what you gone do. I swear I wrote and entire book and then I erased it. I waited till he came to pick me up and I said who is this bitch and why she inboxing me. I don't fucking know her we don't have mutual friends and you must be fucking her too. This the shit I don't like eyes. Then another bitch in boxed me. This nigga was spreading his dick all around Dallas. Man what a stupid ass I was. He just loved pussy not me with his lying ass. He said, Mo I told you what it is and you still told me you loved me. He said I told you that you did not want to be with me. Before I could get it out he said we need to take a break. I swear I laughed. A break nigga? I thought I wasn't ya women. See you confused and fucked up. I can just imagine what you telling these other whores. I said ok cool. I don't think he know me. So I was back on FB doing me. I told him when I wanna fuck I'll call you. He said see that's not cool Mo. I said fuck you and he left.

A few weeks after that, I manage to get and invite FB group called Zay's world. A very raunchy and sexual group that caught my attention daily. But Let me tell you something, that group is where I met that certain someone.....uh uh, don't judge me!!

On to the next chapter....

4

Rough Road Ahead

When I made it home I was sad. It had honestly been the best time of my life in years. I didn't want it to end but back to life back to reality. GOL called me to make sure I made it home safe. He told me how much of a good time he had and I was all he thought I would be and more. He said, I will call you tomorrow because you need to get some rest. I know you got work tomorrow and the gym lol. This cat knew my entire schedule. It was crazy but good. We continued taking and Skyping as usual until one day he called me at work and that's not uncommon. He said Mo, I gotta ask you something. I said, ok what? He said do you trust me. I said yes I do. He said, will you MARRY ME. Without hesitation I said YES. Now I'm sure some of you would be like this was the first time you ever met him and I know this but when it's meant to be it don't take months or years you just know it's real. He was a man who knows what he wanted and that was me.

He made arrangements to move to Dallas in August 24th, 2012 because I was not moving to Chicago. That's kind of cold is not for me. Well honestly he said he never met a women who had been on a job for 12 years so he did not want me to leave my job since I was more stable while he had to find a job when he got down to Dallas. My mom was happy for me even though she had never met him before. She knew her daughter would not bring just anyone to her home. She said I can't wait I meet him. She told me you have to get that house in order for this man. Y'all transparent moment. Ok I still had the box tv's in my house, I had no curtains, I didn't care because nobody came to my house to live with me. It was your typical bachelorette home. I had what I needed. I was not very much of the make it look all nice and home like. I stayed over my moms house until it was time to go to bed so why do all that.

Well anyway me and mom went and got some things to make the house look welcoming for GOL well I'm sure y'all done figured it out by now Michael Burks is GOL/ That special someone. So I will call him by his name now. We bought some food to put in the refrigerator. Hey, I was always over my moms house so I didn't need to cook or buy groceries. I had been single for 6 years so I had to get back in fiancé mode. I thought this was never going to happen again but I was fooled. It looked more like a home I actually lived in once mom was finished with it. She said, now this looks better. He won't be scared when he walks in. I can't stand my mom.

I was skyping with Mike before he came down one day and my daughter ran in because she wanted to see who he was. She heard of him but never seen him. Mike said that's ok. He said, Hello Tyler nice to finally meet you. She said, so you the man making my mom smile again and he just laughed. Well, yes I am and I hope I can make you smile as well. She said ok. I was kinda happy she liked him. Her relationship with her father was rocky so she was not very inviting to anybody that's why I did me but never introduced her to anyone I wasn't serious about.

But anyway Mike was coming down soon so I felt it was time for her to a least see what he looked like. He asked me to cook him Lasagna because it was his favorite food. I said, ok I got you. I didn't know how to to cook it but that Youtube help me out real quick. He told me
I can't wait to see you again and not just for a weekend but for a life time. I said I can't wait either. The days leading up to him coming too Dallas he needed a place to stay because the person who was rooming with could not pay his half of the rent. He didn't want to tell me because he didn't want me to help him. I told him I'm your fiancé and your not going to be on the street so I put him up in a hotel for a few days until his flight left. He said, thank baby you really didn't have to do that. I said I know but I did. He also told me I got a temp job that starts Monday. I said, look at you already got a job lined up. Ok I'm impressed. He said, I gotta make this money. I don't want to be living off you. I have to provide that's what men do right. I said yep. Man for the first time in 6 years I felt loved again. It was a good feeling that God gave me what I asked for. A man who adores me, who wants to take care of me. Who wants to help father my daughter, who goes to church, who actually knows how to lead. I was like..you mean I can be a women for a change. I can't wait! I took care of my first husband and ran the house. I didn't want to go through that again.

The few days past and it was finally time for Mike to come to his new home in Dallas. I was so ready to start my new life. He flew in on a Saturday and I met him at the airport.

We greeted each other with a kiss and a long embrace. I was just smiling and happy for the first time in a longtime. We got his luggage and went to the house. I welcomed him to his new house and the we went over to my moms house. She was only two houses down. We walked in the door and I said, mom here's your son-in-law and they hugged. My mom said glade to see you finally since I heard so much about you. Then I introduced him to my brother and he said what's up man. Welcome to the family and walked off. That's typical of my bro not that welcoming. After my Ex men had to prove themselves to him. Then came Tyler with a big hug and smile she said, hey Dad. My eyes got big because she called him dad. I told you that you don't have to call him dad and she said, I want to mom. Ok that's cool with me. I had to go out of town to a convention in San Antonio, Tx. I was in a direct marketing company at the time so this trip was already paid for in and planned in advance. I did not like leaving him so soon but he understood and besides him and Tyler could get to know each other a little better while I was out of town so for me it worked out just fine.

One of my girlfriends at the time came and picked me up the next day. We drove to San Antonio because it was cheaper. I gave him and Tyler and kiss and he said don't go meet nobody else. I'm like boy please. We laughed and I left. I thought about him the entire ride even though I was holding conversation with my homegirl about the convention. I just was praying him and Tyler was getting along. Once we got to San Antonio, Tx we checked in, got registered, meet up with our National Director and the other team members to strategize on how we will take our business to the next levels. I stayed busy but Mike and I talked when I had breaks and at night. He told me him and Tyler went to a church Carnival and had a lot of fun. He said they are bonding pretty good so don't worry. He said mom is fine as well. I see about her everyday. Wow that was so nice. I was just blushing over the phone. Thank you baby I so appreciate you. He said, naw I appreciate you. Have a good time at the convention. Don't worry I'm taking care of them for you. We will see you when you get home. I said ok.. Love you much. He said, love you too. On the last day of conversation we all went out on the river walk. We went to the karaoke bar had drinks and food. Everybody knew I could sing so they all said come on Mo you gotta sing something. I decided to sing Jill Scott, "is this the way." I decided to call Mike and surprise him with a song. I had a team member hold the phone and I said this is for you baby. Once I was done the entire place stood on there feet and clapped. They gave me high fives and you go girl. I got my phone back and he said thank you baby. I was really missing you but now when you coming home. I said, tomorrow evening. He said hurry up. I just laughed. I Said, Ok.

My team teased me like little kids. They said Mo's gonna get if when she gets home. I said, y'all nasty stop it with a big smile on my face. Anyway, it was time to go home today and I was ready. My fiancé had not been in Dallas but a few days and I had to leave him. I was ready to get back home to with him. The day I arrive home I was greeted by my daughter Tyler and my fiancé Mike. I received hugs and kisses that I was missed. It just felt good to be home. Mikes job was down the street from my job so I had him drop me off and he could go to his job. He gave me a kiss and said see ya later. When he picked me up from work he told me they didn't tell him it was a one day assignment. I told him it was OK you'll find more work don't worry about it. We went home and I cooked him some lasagna. He told me that was good. I just smiled at my Youtube dinner. That's why when chicks say they can't cook they just being lazy because YouTube shows you step-by-step how to cook any dish.

As the week came to an end little did Mike know I was planning a surprise welcome to the Dallas party with all of my closest friends and family this Saturday. It was at one of my church members home. I need a larger space so she was gracious enough to provide her home. She also cooked food and some delicious yummy cake. Let me tell you this women can burn. He ask me what where we doing this weekend and I said, we going to a friends house party and he was like cool I get to meet some of your friends. I also had a real good friend of mine flying in from out of town. That made it that much more special. He only knew of her so him finally meeting others that close to me was good. We got up and got dressed because we had to run some errands earlier that day. It was a beautiful sunny day. He was asking me what should he wear and I said boy its in a house so dress nice but comfortable and it's exactly what he did. He loves for me to wear heels even though they make me very much more taller than he is. That was one thing he loved about me. He knew I was comfortable as long as he was. I had on and oversized shirt some tights and my red heels. I was too cute! He said I love red shoes maybe we can use those later tonight. I giggled and said ok.

So I text to see if everything was ready so we could be on our way and she said yes everything's good. I said, Mike it's time to go you ready? He grabbed the keys and we left. Once we got there he knocked on the door and was greeted by my church member and she said, well hello Michael very nice to meet you Monique has spoken real good things about you she said, I hope so he said yes she did. Y'all come one in. I told everybody he is here my baby Michael and everybody greet him and gave him hugs and welcomed him into the family. Mike said, what's going on Mo. I said just chill. My church member prayed over the food and then we ate.

Everybody was mingling with him while I prepared to talk. I said, attention everyone let me tell you why I asked all of you to join me today. A lot of you may know of Michael but you don't know Michael. He is my lover, my friend, my confident, my fiancé, and my Boaz. He show me how to love when I thought I never wanted to love again. I want asked all of you here today because everyone in this room played a park in my life to help me grow so I wanted you to meet the man I hold dear to my heart and whom I'm about to Marry. I love you baby and I thank God for you every day. Welcome to Dallas and welcome to my family and friends I love you. He was in tears but of joy. He said no one ever made him feel so welcome like you did. He said, I love you too. We ate cake talked more and went home. It was s long day and I was glad it was over. I just wanted to be alone with him for awhile.

It was Sunday morning and we went to church. He got a chance to meet some other people who was not at the party. He also got a chance to meet the pastor of the church who at the time I called my father because I did not have a relationship with my biological father. Pastor told Michael it's was good to see him at church today. He said, we need that to survive and Michael agreed. I was in the church choir so I had to leave my hubby well my soon-to-be hubby in the pew just for a little while. We do praise and worship and I did the announcements and the pastor got up to preach. The sermon was awesome and he gave such a great word but before the service was over he said he had one more announcement. He said Mike you can come up here now. I'm looking like what's going on. He said, well by now you all know my name is Michael Burks and I'm Monique's fiancé. I actually propose to her on the phone while I was in Chicago. I decided that it was only appropriate to propose to her in person. Y'all my face went in my hands and I started to cry. He said, come on up here baby. He grabbed my hand got down on one knee In front of the entire church body and said Monique Moore will you marry me and I said, yes all teary-eyed. Everybody stood up and clapped and that's how the service ended. I was greeted with congratulations from the congregation it was the happiest moment of my life.

I swear I knew God sent me the right one. We immediately started planning and budgeting for the wedding. We looked at venues, Caterers, bands, invitations, guest list, cake.. I mean everything. We started marriage counseling as well. It was so much fun doing this again and with someone who actually didn't leave it all up to me. We wanted to save up for the wedding so we could have it in May of 2012. One day while we was at church my pastor came to us and said since I'm marrying you two would you like to get married after watch night service. We thought that would most definitely cut down on planning for a huge wedding. Mike said it didn't really matter he just wanted to marry me. My pastor said don't worry about decoration, cake etc we will take care of it. We just need you two to show up. We agreed and the date was set 12/31/11 at Midnight which made it 1/1/12.

One of Ladies from church ask me have you purchased your wedding dress yet and I said no I have been looking but have not found anything to my liking. She said, how about I make the dress for you. I was like oh my God thank you so much. That really removed the stress of trying to try on a bunch of dress. We went to the pattern store to pick out fabric. I had already been married before so I just chose an off white cream color. I'm simple and I'm not a bridezilla. This was all coming together and I was so thankful for everyone helping plan our wedding at no charge. It's was meant to be. The day of the wedding I was nervous.

We woke up ready to get it in motion. We both ran around making sure last minute stuff was taken care of all day and we would meet at the church. Once we got there for watch night service it was on. In a few hours we would be husband and wife. As the service came close to an end Mike and I left the sanctuary to get dressed. While this was happening they was transforming it into a beautiful place for our wedding. I was so nervous but ready to be a wife again. They called for me to come because it was time to get stared with the ceremony. None of Mikes family could make it to the wedding so he had stand ins. The pastors wife stood in for his mom and the pastors son was the best man. I tell you my christian family went above and beyond for him. My mom was there for the lighting of the candle. The man who gave me away was like a father to me so that was special. My daughter was there, my brides maids and some of my other family, members of church and friends. I was surprised so many people came. It's was New Years so you know people be getting they drink and party on. They wasn't trying to be at a wedding.

So the music started to play and one of Mikes favorite songs was "If only you knew" by Patti Labelle. This was my que to start walking toward the entrance. Once I got there they rolled out the wedding runner for me to walk on. I looked down and saw my hubby smiling at me. As the song faded out they started to play She by Eric Roberson. It was my time. They pastor said can everyone stand and I stared to walk down the aisle. I was so happy it was time. I noticed my hubby started to cry and I almost cried but I held my composure. I didn't want to mess up my makeup not yet anyway. The music died down, I took his hand and the pastor started the wedding. Once he was done with his part then Mike and I made our own wedding vowels.

Mike went first.. these were his vows,

"2 years, 8 months and 31 days. That's 900 days 37500 hours and that was the first day I met you until this point. every minute, every second, of my life has been the most exciting journey I've ever taken. And I keep thinking it's just not over yet. Whatever it is you do, keep doing it. Matter of fact start all over again so I can revisit how you touched my soul. The only fear is that you will mistaken my simple affections as just that. I kiss you only in the attempt to breath the same air you breath. I hug you close only to occupy the same space as you and I look into your eyes just so I can see the same sites you see. I wish I was a kit kat so I could break you off a piece of me so you could never be without me again. (everyone was in awe at this point) Now for the best part. I promise from
This day forth I will take care of you spiritually, Emotionally, mentally and physically. I will be careful to follow God's instructions cause I know my lead you will follow. You heart is safe with me safer with me than any object I have ever owned in my life. As for your spirt I will be careful to

help you prepare for the day that you and me step in the heavily gates. I love you I cherish you and it is my goal to find new ways to make you smile in each and every moment of my life and I live you. Y'all need to see the video because I melted like butter and was hot like fire lol. As I was crying I said boy and everyone laughed. You gone mess up my makeup.

Now it was my turns after I cooled down. I went on to say…

"Michael when I met you 2 years ago on Facebook never did I think I would be standing hère today before you saying I vowed to spend the rest of my life with you. I was not wanting any parts of love because I had shut the door on it but God has another plan. He showed me my best friend, my leader and my lover, a teacher and my backbone. You blew life into a soul that was lost. I feel so free of the damage that was done to me Years ago. We think we know what love is like. Love has no look. It just comes along when you are willing to accept it. I honor you. I appreciate all that you have brought to my life and all that you will continue to bring to our family. I thank God for you every day. I love you for the man you are now and the man you will be and i will always remain faithful to you. I love you. "

We repeated after pastor and exchanged rings. He pronounced us man and wife and before we kissed they handed Mike a step stool so he could be taller than me and the crowed laughed so hard. We was husband and wife. It was finally done. They gave us a beautiful reception. It was the beginning of a new life

So I thought as the first year past all was good in the Burks home. We was getting along good. We decided to try to have a baby. We had talked about it and we both wanted another one. I always wanted a son so I was ready. After months of trying I got pregnant. I was so excited and so was Mike. He always wanted a big family. He was at all my doctors appointments and he always took good care of me. We watched the sonogram of the baby looking like the size of s pea. I was so happy. I thought I was too old to have children. One day we went to the doctors appointment for a sonogram and as the tech was checking I didn't see anything. I became worried immediately. Mike said baby all is well don't worry. I was like ok. The tech said the doctor need to come in and talk with us. When the doctor came in she said hello Mr. & Mrs. Burks I'm sorry to inform you that you had a miscarriage. I was devastated. I became numb and was just ready to go. I started blaming myself and thinking that I couldn't have children anymore but that was not the case. I was healthy and the doctor said these things can happen with any woman at any age. I understand but I was still upset. I told Mike maybe it's just not in God's plan for us to have a baby. So I didn't focus on it much but that didn't mean we didn't stop practicing lol.

I had to have a DNC done to remove what was left of the fetus. It was kinda heart breaking but my man got me through it and the recovery as well. It was just one of those things that happened. It was nothing wrong with me and I had to understand that. We kept trying and it finally happened. I had a pretty good pregnancy this 2nd go around and baby Matthew Burks was Born June 15, 2013 via c-section. We was so excited and happy. I finally got my son. We came home with him 5 days later. All was well.

During this time my daughter Tyler stayed with my mom sometimes during the week and Mike said she needed to stay with us more so we could be a family. So we told Tyler she could only spend the night over moms house on the weekends. Tyler was not happy about that and did not like it but I agreed with him. She went and told my mom what we was going to do so mom came over to the house and asked us why. We said, Tyler gets away with a lot of stuff and that has to stop especially with that cell phone. That was one reason she needed to be in our presence daily.

Mom was like Mike Tyler is my grandchild and you telling me when she can stay and not stay is unacceptable. Mike told my mom no disrespect but this piece of paper shows I'm married to your daughter and so I'm the man of this house and Tyler's needs to be here during the week. My eyes got big because for the first time I did not and can not side with her. Tyler needed to be watched because we had no idea what she was doing on that cell phone and mom did not understand that. She told Mike DAMN YOUR WEDDING LICENSE. Monica is my daughter and you are not taking her away from me and Tyler. I put Matthew in the bassinet still sore walked to the bedroom door and said mom don't do that. Let me remind you I still had staples in my stomach from my c-section and was not supposed to be out of bed. That's not cool at all. She looked at me and walked out the door. I felt bad but what we was doing was right.

Let me give you some background really quick, Mike has 15 years experience in IT and he knew social media like the back of his hand. We needed to have Tyler close to us. I knew she was doing something but I could never catch her. This is when things with Tyler and my Mike went south.

Mike started checking Tyler's cell phone randomly. One day he was at work and he was on his iPad. He went into his pictures to find a picture that he needed. There was some photos that was loading while he was scrolling to find what he needed. I don't know what he did but Tyler's pictures was coming to his iPad. I was on my way taking her and her sister to the nail shop when I received a phone call from Mike. He said, "what you doing"? I said on my way to the nail shop with the girls. He said, "turn the car around and go home". I was like OK is everything all right he? He said, "I will talk to you when I get home". So when I got home Mike pull out his iPad and showed me pictures of my daughter that was inappropriate. I beat the breaks off Tyler's ass. She was only fourteen. I took her phone and grounded her for a month. She told Mike she hated him and this was his fault. She said, I wish he would have never came here. Stop trying to be my dad. It was down hill from there. It did not matter what I did or said to her. She would be ok for minute and then go back to her old ways lying, sneaking out, bringing boys in my house all kinds of shit that should've got her ass beat.

My mom just felt he was to controlling when actually he was just trying to run the house like a husband should. They both were just use to it only be us. Change is hard but it is needed and I understood it as Mike's wife. Hell it was even hard for me but I learned to adjust. As time went by it was an up and down battle with my mom and Tyler but I stood my ground with them. I can see the frustration in Michael's face daily because he was trying so hard to get them to understand that he is the leader of this home and what we says goes. I have his back period. I told my mama you run your house how you see fit and we'll run our house how we see fit it's really that simple. She didn't agree but she understood and told me ok you are right. I will do my best to stay out of your business.

The daily stress from my Mike and my daughter put a toll on our marriage where we would argue every other day. He became a little distant. I knew something was up. So I asked God to reveal to me what I need to see. I normally don't go through Mikes stuff but once day he left his messenger open and I saw some conversations with a young lady that was not appropriate for a married man to be discussing. I was pissed off on all levels but I needed more information. I went through his Facebook messenger and saw more message from other women. I also went through his email and saw a conversation with a women he worked with. I was devastated and broken. I was so tired of giving my all to men and they end up being disloyal. I confronted him with the information I found and of course he tried to lie the first time about it like all men do when they caught. Then he blamed me for his actions. That bullshit did not work on any level. He did not sleep with anyone but the fact he was talking to them as if he was single was enough for me.

He finally confessed and he apologized for his actions but I was still wounded. We decided to see our pastor for council. I saw that he still loved me and he wanted to work it out so I agreed because I'm sure I played a part in what happen. Some might not agree with this but it's how I felt. Sometimes we as women drop the ball as well. I just wanted to know why he felt the need to do what he did and maybe I can get a better understanding so it won't happen again.

While we attended council I noticed my mother was going to the doctor a lot more than normal. I decided to have a talk with her. I said, mom what's going on. I don't want a repeat of you not telling me if something is wrong. She said Monica the tumor is back. I was like ok so what's the game plan? She said, don't know yet. I said, well I'm going to all doctor appointments with you so I can be in the loop. She agreed so I had to alter my work schedule to be there for her. When I went to the doctor appointment I made sure I asked many questions. I needed to have a clear understanding of what was going on with my mom and the treatment involved. They did a lot of X-rays, MRI's and cat scans to get a clear game plan for the treatment.

Meanwhile my brother Charles was was mowing the lawn on day and fell out. He had to be rushed to the hospital and we found out he had Leukemia. It just seem everybody was getting sick. My brother's illness was more self inflicted. He's an alcoholic and has been told many times to stop drinking but he didn't so the Leukemia stay around longer. It was just a trying time for our family but I stayed strong with my main VIP Mike. He always had my back even when I felt like I had to do this by myself.

When I left to go to work in the mornings I would always stop and check on my mom to see if she needed anything and if she was ok. Since the diagnosis she was doing well. Once all the X-rays came back they said mom would need a biopsy. This is when they stick a camara down your nose to take a closer look at the tumor so they can properly treat it. I was worried for her but as always my mom said I will be fine Monica. I've done this twice before remember. I said, you write mom. You got this. You gone beat it again. They set up the appointment for the same week and we went back in early morning to have the procedure done.

While she was in recovery the doctor came out and told us that she needed radiation and chemo treatment ASAP so she agreed but she clearly told them I will not go through a 3rd operation to remove this tumor. She always told me she was not doing it a 3rd time but my mom was a fighter and she was going to fight like she always has.

She began treatment that was called a cyber knife. It was more advance in shrinking tumors. She was always tired afterwards but didn't stay down for long. She continued her everyday life as if nothing was wrong. One day I came over before work and as I entered her room I saw a lot of bloody tissues on the floor along with a towel. I was like mom, what the hell! Why didn't you call me? She said, "it's just a little blood". I said, really mom. Get yo ass up we gong to emergency. Now remind you I never spoke to my mom like that but if you all saw what I saw you would have cussed as well. I called into my job and said I had to take my mom to the emergency room. She was bleeding from last night all the way to the emergency room. I was scared as hell. We got there and they rushed her to the back. They did a method called packing where they put these special gauze in her nose to stop the bleeding and it did. I was like thank you God. They stabilized her and she was able to go home. I was like mom please don't do that again. You should have called me. I didn't want to bother you and Mike. I was like mom really your my mother you can bother me whenever. She apologized and all was well.

We went to the next doctors appointment and all seemed well. He said the cyber knife was shrinking the tumor so she just needed to continue treatment. He said the blood issues was a side effected of the biopsy but she still looks good. That gave me some peace of mind for a little while. Mom started to stumble a lot more that usual. Her equal librium was alway off since the first head surgery but it became more aggressive. She began to complain about the tooth she had been having issues with about 2 years. I was like mom go get that tooth taken out. It was causing her headaches and a host of other issues so she finally got an appointment to get it taken out.

While she was waiting for that my brother Charles ended up in the hospital again behind his leukemia. His platelets was very low. It was so low that it can cause blood clots. He also needed to be treated for his alcoholism so it was a dangerous time for him. He had to be admitted to the hospital for awhile and that was good because at least he can get the help he needed. I would go to the hospital to follow up and talk with the doctors for him on top of taking care of mom and working my full time job. It was stressful at times but I had to take care of my family.

I was at work one day when I got a call from out neighbor. She said, Monica your mom was taken by ambulance to the hospital. I was like what's wrong. She said, your mom was having real bad headaches. She could not stand. I was like ok where is she going. She said, to Methodist. I said why, her medical files are at UT southwest. I was like

I'm leaving work now and thank you. I called Mike at his job and told him what was happening. He said, you need me to come to the hospital? I said naw let me find out what's up first and then I'll call you. He said, ok. I told my job my mom was in the emergency and left. I drove like a bat out of hell from Irving to Dallas. I made it to emergency and asked for my mother. I went to the room and Mrs Pat from down the street was in the ER with my mom. I immediately ask mom what's wrong. She said, Monica my head is killing me. It just hurts so bad. So I went to the nurse and asked them what's going on? What are y'all doing for my mother headache. He said, we are waiting on the ER doctor to put the order in. I said, how long does that take she is in pain. He said let me go check.

I swear I was about to cuss these nurses out. She had been there 30 min before I arrived. Anyway I went back to moms bedside and she said, Monica I need to pee. I said, on let me help you. Mrs Pat and I took her to the restroom and she needed me to help her because she could not stand on her own. I knew then it was more serious than a headache. Once she was done I took her back to the bed. I was just watching her and then she said Monica, come here. I walked to her bedside. She said, "MONICA I THINK IM MY WAY OUT OF HERE." I said, mom don't say that. You're gonna be fine ok. I was about to go get that nurse again and he walked in with her pain medicine. They gave her morphine for her pain. She looked fine because she was at rest and not hurting anymore. As I sat there and watched her she started to breath funny. I called her name and she was unresponsive. I started to shake her and she wouldn't wake up or respond. I went and got the nurse who gave her the medicine. I asked him should she be breathing like that and he said no. He tried to wake her as well and nothing happened. He went and got the ER doctor and he orders a medicine that reverses the affects of the morphine to wake her up and nothing happen. Her blood pressure shot up to 223/106. She was going into cardiac arrest so they rushed me out of the room. He ordered a cat scan of her brain. While hat was happening I called Michael and told him I needed him. He asked what's wrong and I was frozen. He said, Im coming baby. While I waited on him the doctor came in and said it's not the morphine it's something going on with her brain. I'm sorry but your mom had a brain aneurysm and went into cardiac a-rest. She is dying. I'm sorry Mrs Burks. I was shock. I could not believe what he just told me and I became numb.

Mike walked into the ER and I just looked at him. He said, baby what's wrong. I just looked at him and he knew. He just hugged me. He went to the doctor and they told him what happen. I just looked at him in disbelief. I just started calling the family. I didn't have time to cry. I had work to do. Mike was like baby it's going to be ok. I just looked at him with a blank look. We was going to counseling for his infidelity, my brother is in the hospital and now my mom is dying. I did not give fuck about nothing. I hated God and I was suffering inside because I felt there was something I missed. This is not happening. I really felt it was all a dream.

I called my job to inform them of what happen to my mom and told them I was not coming back to work for now. They informed me that they understood. The doctor told me they was waiting on a room for my mom. Family started showing up but I was still numb. I just didn't believe she was dying. They finally got her up to the room. Her and my brother was on the same floor in the same hospital. He had already been there for a month because of his Leukemia. I was like really God. You gone take both of them away. The floor they was on in the hospital is were either you were dying or you can die any day. Mom was at the end of the hall and Charles was at the top of the hall.

I went into the room and told Charles what was happening and he was in disbelief as well. He got the nurse to bring him down to the room to see mom. Then he told them to take him back. He just couldn't stand to see her like that. Mike tried to get me to leave to get some fresh air but I couldn't so he went to get stuff from the house for me. I slept at the hospital and he stayed with me. Everybody came to see mom. They was as shocked as I was. It was hard seeing her like that. The doctor asked me did I want to take her off life support. This was hard but my mom told me if this ever happened that I needed to let her go. She said she did not want to be like a vegetable. She was brain dead so there was no coming back from it. I told him

yes you can take her off. After everyone left they removed
the life support.

My mom was so strong. She kept on breathing like a
champ. She just looked like she was sleeping. I was by
her bedside and sometimes sleeping beside her. I was
walking down to Charles room to visit him and talk and to
see who how his recovery was going. He was so cool
when he was not drinking. We was reminiscing and talking
about mom. It was good therapy for both of us. Mike got
me to leave the hospital for a minute just to go to Walmart.
I really didn't want to go but he insisted that I needed to
get some fresh air. We made our way back and I went to
take a shower. I heard someone call my name as clear as
day. I looked out the door and ask Mike did you call me, he
said no baby I didn't. I said Mike somebody called me I'm
not crazy. He said, I know baby. It was my mom Mike. I
know it was and he said then it was. I finished drying off
and walked down to Charles room for a little bit. Charles
room phone rang and the nurse told me my mom
had died.

I rushed down to her room and just looked at her. She had
a tear rolling down her eye with her mouth slightly open…
she was gone. I knew then when I heard her call my name
it was her telling me she was leaving me to go home to
our father. That her time was up. They wheeled Charles
down and we just sat at her bedside and just looked at
her. The women that gave us life was gone May 5, 2014

RIP Cynthia MacFadden Roberts. I love you Queen. I will miss you forever.

Well..It was time to plan her funeral. My brother Charles still had to stay in the hospital due to his platelets still being dangerously low. He said do what you gotta do. Momma made you the queen so handle business like I know you will. I was in work mode so no time for mourning. I was thankful I had lots of help from more friends than family. My mom was a Queen/Boss. She had a pre-paid burial that was paid for. She always told me when she died she never wanted me and Charles to worry about that part. She took care of business in life and death. I went to Golden Gate with my husband and we started the proceeding. It was fairly easy to do. My pastor who married Mike and I allowed us to have the service at the church. Everyone just came together to help me through this trying time. I was never alone but I felt like it at times. As the planning continued I was still going to the hospital to see about my brother. The doctor allowed him to leave the day before the funeral. He told me he had to come back the next day so they could check his platelets count. One of the ladies at my church was a nurse and told me she would be on standby for my brother. They had the choir section roped for him. He could not be in contact with anyone. I told her thank you so much. The day of the funeral It was a sunny and beautiful outside. I was so numb but I had work to do. I took Charles back to the hospital to get tested. The doctor admitted him. He said his platelets was just too low. My brother said go bury our mom I love you. My heart just dropped. Can you imagine how that would make you feel. He could not go pay his respect to his mother. I got you Bro.. I went home and got ready to go to the church.

As I road in the limo all I could do was think about my mom. The numb feeling just continued. I didn't want to feel. Once we arrived I got out of the car holding my husbands hand tight. My knees got weak for a minute but I regained my composure. Everything looked beautiful even my mother. The service was beautiful and well put together. My favorite part was when my baby Tyler praise dance for her grannie to "Take me to the King" by Tamela Mann. It was a beautiful tribute to her. My mom was crazy about her. She broke down toward the end but her fellow dancers rallied around her and loved on her and so did I. My pastor did the eulogy and then it was over. I payed my last respect to her and closed the casket May 10, 2014 was the last time I laid eyes on my mom.

Moving forward I was lost, hurt, confused, angry, mad at God. My emotions was all over the place but I didn't want to feel so I shut them all down. I went back to work as usual. I didn't take FMLA. I just kept going full force not dealing with my issues. Charles was home after 2 month stay in the hospital. He was sober and looking good. I was so happy to see him. He was happy to be home as well. He hates hospitals. I prayed he would stay sober and not turn back to the bottle.

Charles's birthday rolled in and I bought him a record player so he could listen to his vinyl records. I bought him the Purple Rain album by Prince. Y'all he loved that movie. I mean he had to have it on VHS, DVD & cassette tape. He would play it so much until he had to buy another. He loved his car and washed that thang almost every day. He even gave it a name ..Kitty lol. I would go watch TV with him from time to time. Anything to keep him from wanting to drink but it just didn't work. He was doing so good and then he relapsed a month later. He was missing mom and he felt he had no one any more. I told him you got me but I guess that's not what he wanted. He became wreck-less and not caring about anything.

There where times when he was so drunk he would fall out in the house. I would have to go over and help him to the bed. He drank every day. He was picking fights, talking crazy to people. It was like he wanted to die. He ended up in and out of the hospital. I had to make sure his bills got paid. It's was like taking care of another child. He refused to go the the doctor sometimes but I made his ass go. The doctors would tell him time and time again Mr. Roberts you need to stop drinking but he wouldn't listen. He said I'm gonna do what I want.

It seemed like once or twice a month he would end up at the ER. One time he had to be detoxed so bad that once he came down he ended up having a seizure. I was scared because I was in the room with him when it happen. When they released him he was on about 7 different medication. He did not do what he was supposed to do. He would mix the medicine with alcohol which just made him sicker. This same behavior went on for year. He had one episode with his withdrawal that he didn't know where he was. It hurt me to see him in so much pain. I tried to get him to seek counseling and he wouldn't.

One day he woke up and his neck was swollen so big none of his pain meds would work. The tumor on this throat has gotta bigger so they needed to do a biopsy on it. While he was in recovery the doctor came out and said he needs to get started on chemo and radiation so we can shrink this tumor. I set up the appointments and I had to take him because he wouldn't go on his own. It was like deja vu. He went to see the same doctors that my mom did. It put me in a mental space I did not want to be in so I suppressed it. I didn't have time to feel. I had to take care of my brother. During all this time he continued to drink. I tried my best to stop him but he was on a mission to drink himself to death. It was hurtful to see him like that. He did chemo one time and decided he only wanted radiation. It was a constant battle with him but I would win most of the time because I would have to threaten him by not talking to him and he didn't like that. I was all he had and honestly the only person that would tolerate his honoree ass.

One day I woke up to a phone voicemail that he was in the hospital. He normally calls me to take him to the emergency room but he didn't this time. I got up and raced up there. I got there and was fussing at him for not calling me. He apologized but said it was in the middle of the night. It was just easier to call the ambulance. A doctor walked in and said you must be his sister. I said yes. She said let me talk with you outside. I said bro I will be back. She said, Mr Roberts Cancer has metastasized. It's in his lungs, tail bone and throat. He only has 6 moths to live. I just looked at her for a moment and said ok and thank you. She said, all we can do is make him comfortable with meds. He can also get some radiations if needed but I don't recommend it. I said, ok again and thank you.

I went back in and talked to him. I said, you know what's up and he said yes but don't count me out sis. I'm gone fight and I said I know you will because our mom did. The radiation doctors tried to give him a dose of radiation for his hip pain but it was so bad that I told them it's not going to work leave him be. He was in too much pain. They took him back to his room and we prepared for discharge. They had an ambulance to bring him home on hospice care.

May 25th the reality kicks in that I only have 3 to 6 months to be with my brother. The nurses came over, social worker, and they delivered a bed for him. Although it is a little overwhelming I stayed strong like mama did when she moved my Aunt Faye into her home and took care of her. She had died of breast cancer some time back. He was happy to be home but the night hit and things changed. He was up most of the night confused but aware of his surrounding. He said, Monica I'm sorry and I told him don't be. We gone do this together.

May 26th-the day started off with the nurse coming by to show me how to do his feeding tube. It's wasn't hard seeing I did my mother's feeding tube before. She showed me how to give him his pain meds. She was a very nice women. She did hospice care for a living. She said the best thing for him is to keep him comfortable and as happy as you can.

May 27th- I did not get much sleep that night. Charles woke up at 1:30am and then at 4am. We took a picture together and he tells me to wait and he picks up this bell that I gave him to call me when he needed help getting out of bed. He was acting silly and I loved that about him. He sat up smoked a cigarette and then he said I want a filet-O-Fish sandwich from McDonald's. Mike went and got it for him. After he ate only a few bites he went back to sleep. I can only imagine what my brother's thoughts was. My only thing was I just didn't want him to suffer. I wanted him to enjoy the time he had left.

I wanted to reach out to my father but I was being stubborn for awhile. I was still holding a grudge against him for not being there when my mom died. I just didn't care but deep down I knew I was wrong so I called my mentor Karen or Pretty Girl K as I call her. She told me Mo, it's not about you it's about Charles. Reach out to your dad for his sake and if he don't show up then you have done your part. Man that Queen always showed me the light when I was in my anger and I totally love her for that.

So I called on a friend who I knew went to the same church as my father did. I told him what was going on with my brother and he said I got you Mo. I hate what's happening to your brother. He was always cool with me. I said thank you. He said I have your father's number. He gave it to me and I told him thank you. I just looked at the damn number in anger. His holly ass done gave everybody else his number but his ONLY FUCKING daughter and son don't have it. He calls his self a man of God. That's some man of bullshit. Y'all I got bipolar for a second. I was In rage but then I came back down and remembered why I was doing this. I told Mike Im scared to call because of possible rejection. Mike
said "hell I'll call him, I want to see this man period". So he called and he didn't answer. I said see typical ass. Mike said, baby give him a chance to call. I said ok cool.

I was exhausted so I didn't write on 5/28. So we will skip to 5/29/17. It was a long day as usual. People came over to visit Charles. His long time best friend Jay Terry, his brother Craig Terry, Will another high school friend, my friend Renee, Lois a long time Aunt to the family. She was my moms friend forever. My cousin Ray Ray and his wife. I mean everybody came by. He noticed some people and some he did not. The cancer was eating away at his memory and breaking him down. It was hard to see something but I hung in there..

5/30/17- He woke up about 4:15am and we just listen to his records. We was jamming a little and he would smile. He had a hard time with words but I could understand what he wanted to say. He would watch a little TV and sleep on and off. He was still smoking his cigarettes but one half of one. I could tell he was going down day by day.

5/31/17- He slept most of the day away. We didn't talk at all. He would just look at me and try to talk but he couldn't. I would hold his hand and talk to him. My pain ran deep but I knew I can't cry. All I could do is watch the life leave my brother. I went over to the house to be relieved for work and Mike would come over and take the day shift. We switch out because I could not afford to not work so I worked from home everyday running on empty. I was barley getting any sleep. It's was just hard as fuck. Can you imagine day in day out watching someone you love die. I fucking hate cancer and what it has done to my family. The Chaplin and social worker came by. We all talked and we prayed over Charles and read scriptures. It was actually nice. I needed a sign from God because I sure as hell did not like him.

6/1/17-It's a new month and I'm so glad May is gone. It's a New month. My brother is still here fighting. He slept a lot today. We had to up how meds because this tailbone pain increased. He woke up for a little while. He pointed and me and I walked over. He wanted a hug. Then he pointed at Mike and he hugged him. I actually teared up. Charles and Mike argued a lot because he really didn't like Mike. Hell he really don't like nobody lol but he let Mike know that he was thankful for him helping out. One day I played my new song Shout In the Name of God for him. He smiled but went back to sleep. It's was good to see him smile instead of in pain. I see why God delayed me dropping my single. I had to prepare to sing it at my brothers funeral.

6/2/17-Charles started to sleep more and more. We had to double up on his meds to keep him comfortable. My dad was supposed to come by today to see his son. My brother is 49 and we can't remember the last time we saw our father. I hope this gives my brother the peace he could not get on earth. My cousin came by to give Mike and I a break. I didn't want to leave but I had to go get some air. All I did was work, stay in the house with Charles everyday all day. I just needed a breather. It felt good to just be with my husband alone.

6/3/17- My dad called and said he was coming over. It took him long to respond and come over because he was healing from pneumonia. My husband said I see where all this height came from. Your daddy tall as hell. I remember telling Mike I was gone cuss him out when I saw him. He stepped to the door and I looked and him and just started crying. My dad came out and held his arms out. I went to him and we embraced. I felt safe in his arms for the first time in my 40 years of my life. All I ever wanted was for him to hold me and tell me it's going to be ok and he did.

He said, daddies here baby. Then he dropped his head and walked into Charles room. Mike looked over at me and said "cotton candy.. soft ass. Yeah Mo you cussed his ass out." I just started laughing.

6/4/17-Charles is heavily medicated for comfortably. He is not eating or smoking now. He has a feeding tube set up to automatically feeds him. Jay came over this morning and stayed with Charles while I went to make arrangements so when he does pass all will be taken car of. We went to Waffle
House to ear because Mike was making sure I ate but I just took a few bites and couldn't eat anymore. I was depressed y'all. The reality kicked in that Charles was dying.

6/5/17-Today the nurse said it was time to put Charles on 24 hour nurse care. He was shutting down. I just felt sick to my stomach. I can't say, my chest started to hurt, I'm tired. I'm just at a lost for words today.

6/6/17 & 6/7/17- I
didn't want to write. I was in my feeling.

6/8/17-Charles is not looking good. I have been talking to him on and off all day. I played music for him. I talked about mom. It was just random stuff. The nurse said he could hear me. I knew he was listening. He was so small. I could see the life leaving him.

6/9/17-Today Charles woke up and was alert, they call this a Rally. It happens before they are about to pass away. I grabbed his hand and told him momma was waiting on him and I would be fine. I said, I love you. He squeezed my hand and that was confirmation he heard me. I sat at his bedside and cried inside. I only had one sibling y'all. It's was just me and Charles. My mom was gone. It's wasn't supposed to be like this. They was supposed to be here to see Addi & Matthew grow up. This is was not fair at all. My entire immediate family was gone in a matter of years. All I had left was my dad and I was still on the fence about that. Why did you bring him back now lord. Why? I'm just confused and hurt. But the reality is this would be my las time seeing him alive.

6/10/17-That final call. It was 4:30 AM and something told me to go to my phone. I saw 3 missed called from the hospice nurse. I called her and said what's wrong. She said Mrs Burks I'm sorry but Mr. Roberts has passed away. I just turned and looked at Mike and said Noooooo. I put on my clothes and ran down to the house. I grabbed his hand and stood over him and kissed his head as I did many morning and nights. No more suffering. No more pain. You can finally rest. I love you Charles Edward Roberts Jr. There is no one like you. Until we meet again. I only want to see you laughing in that purple rain.

5

EmpowerHer Was Birthed

It's been 4 years since my mother passed away and It's been a year and 3 months since My brother passed away. I have some good days and some bad days with accepting that they are gone. For a longtime I actually felt like my mother would walk through the door and I would wake up from this madness in my brain. I never had time to heal from her death so my bothers death was still fresh. I bottled my pain up because I felt I had to move on because my family needed me. I was dead ass wrong. All I was doing was existing and not living.

I went back to work without skipping a beat. It was hard because I was use to talking to my mom and then when she died I would call and talk to my brother. I just did what I had to do. I didn't care about anything really. I lost the love to do a lot of things but with the help of my husband Mike, my daughters Tyler and Deleoris and my son Matthew I pushed through it daily.

After awhile I started to not be able to focus at work. I was snappy, mad at everything. I couldn't sleep, eat or think straight. I started to have dizzy spells, black outs, headaches and a bunch of other stuff. I knew something was wrong but in my head I had to keep going. I didn't have time to grieve. I went to the doctor and she diagnosed me with Depression and Anxiety. I didn't want medication but she told me it was needed so instead of being against it I took the meds. I also ended up having a mild heart attack in the midst of all that. I didn't even know I was having one to be honest. I wen to the doctor for chest pains and they did an EKG on me and that's how I really found out.

I was literally falling apart but I couldn't see it. I felt I was fine and everybody else was on bullshit. I took most of my anger out on my husband. They say you hurt the one that is close to you and that was Mike. I finally decided to take FMLA (family medical leave act) since I did not take it for my moms death or Charles death. I needed a break and I qualified for it. I felt maybe with some time off I would be good but boy was I wrong so wrong.

I fell into a deep dark depression. Mike and I fought damn near every day. The fact that I was not dealing with my grief well was tearing my husband and I apart. I wouldn't hurt my children but I didn't give a damn about hurting Mike. That's some dirty shit to say but at that time that's how I felt. It had nothing to do with him though. I was just hurting and wanted him to hurt as well.

That's was fucked up on all levels but that's what I did. Finally one day Mike with tears in his eyes looked at me and said, Mo you gotta get some help baby. I love you but I can't keep allowing you to abuse me like this. The way he looked at me and the fact that my husband NEVER CRIES showed me I was fucking up and was about to be a a divorced women made me see help.

I began to see a grief councilor. She visited me at my home many times when my brother was alive. We had some sessions and I would cry it out but apparently my pain was deeper than my mom and brothers death. I decided to seek a therapist for mental disorders. This was hard for me. I have always been a strong women. I have always bounced back no matter what the situation. I didn't want to show signs of weakness. That's not me. I would put my own feeling aside to make sure everyone else got what they needed. I struggled in the beginning with my therapy because I was in denial that I had issues but once I opened up I found out I had a severe case of PTSD (post traumatic stress syndrome). Once she broke it down I was like well damn that's why I'm on 10 all the damn time on top of me holding everything in.

I had to see my therapist because I could not function properly so since I needed some type of income. I chose to apply for short term disability because my doctor would not release me to go back to work. That shit was stressful because of shit they put you through for the little bit of money they give you is awful. It's sad because I paid for it for 18 plus years. You would think it would not be this hard to get. How crazy does that sound… but anyway.

Meanwhile life still had to go on. Later on at some point Mike had joined this coaching group called Grindation and I was just supporting him. I had no interest in being involved. It's was a group for women and men entrepreneurs. I did not do women so I didn't want to join

As a few years passed by they added a women's division called the Gwomen. Mike told me you are joining because you need some women in your life. I told him I don't trust or do women you know that. He said, and that's why you need to join. You have to get around woman who understand other women Mo. The only reason I joined is because of one women and her name is Karen my Pretty girl K. I gave her that nick name because I called her husband Kendall Pretty boy Ken lol. She was the first women in a long time I felt I could trust besides my mother. I told her things that's I normally would only tell my mom. We found out we had so much more in common so when Gwomen was developed I was on board with joining because she was the Queen who was the leader of this community.

We had daily video conference calls. I got a chance to meet and bond with some dope ass women. We all just bonded because we all where real about our issues. I thought I was going through my stuff until I heard some of the other women stories. It was good to be in a community where people wasn't fake. We helped each other and everyone was able to give advice about any situation. I felt valued for once in a longtime. We all had something to offer our sisters. We are our sisters keeper. We had our very first women's retreat in Bonita Springs, Florida last June of 2018. I was not sure I was going to make it but God always steps in and gives you what he knew I needed…. a get away/vacation.

I was blessed with a ticket round trip by an awesome sister. I was so excited because it's was a place I had never been before.

It was so nice to see all my Gwomen in the flesh. We was so use to seeing each other on a video call. We all hugged and got checked into the rooms, we got our agendas, talked and got to know each other. The next day was class sessions that got very personal and deep. We had to deal with some stuff and some issues and the way they had it set up you was gonna face your issues willingly. I was holding back honestly but a real sister will call you on your shit because she knows you're good at masking your hurt. Everybody was going around the table speaking there truth being vulnerable and I was there as a sister being compassionate to them.

It's was my turn and I was really fighting my emotions y'all. I didn't want to let go oh but let me tell you how God uses people. There was this one sister Mel B. She stood at the end of the round table looked me in my face and said Mo it's not your fault. You did everything you could to save your mother. I just broke down. She came to where I was and she lifted my head and said oh no ma'am you hold your head up. Everybody in that room surrounded me and they said LET IT GO MO. I just screamed and said Oh God. I had been holding that pain ever since my mom died. I felt like there was something else I could have done to save her. That guilt is what was killing me inside, making me lash out at

My husband, and all the other shit I was doing. I finally decided that day to let it go. My sisters played a big part in my healing process. I love all of you so much. I was never the same after that weekend. I felt for the first time since mom died I could trust women again. I love my Gwomen.

Moving forward to the end of the year my husband and I decided to go to Grindfest in Atlanta. This is a s business and entrepreneur conference held by my husbands coach and founder of Grindation Kendall Ficklin. I had never been to one before and I also had never been to Atlanta this was a new experience for me. We packed the kids up and got on the road. We got to ATL and went straight to the Airbnb. Then we went downtown to the Marriott and registered for the event. It was good seeing the women and the men under one roof. It was a weekend jammed pack with knowledge, fellowshipping, couple Council, single council. I don't think there was a topic we did not touch on. We had break out session for women only, then the men and group sessions. It's was just real and raw and I totally enjoyed myself. On the last day it was awards day. We had a great dinner, fellowship & fun. There was an award ceremony and it was time for what was called the Gwomen of the year award. This was the first time this award was ever given out. Karen or Pretty girl K started taking about this person and how they would getting knock down but come back swing, how resilient they were, strong etc and I was thinking of all the women I thought that would get the award and to my surprise that women was ME. I just put my hands in my face and cried.

I couldn't believe it. My husband was yelling "let's Go baby". I was so excited. That was the way to end the weekend.

One my way home I just got to brainstorming and my husband said what's next Women of the Year. I said, I don't know and he said yes you do. It's time for your to tell your story. It's time to help other women. It's time to EmpowerHER. That was how the EmpowerHER Queendom was Born.

It' was Born off of my pain, struggles, PTSD, anxiety, the death of my mom & my brother. It was born to show you ladies, you Queens that no matter how far or deep you fall in a hole you can crawl your way out into greatness. You can become a person you never saw yourself as. You can not be ashamed of what you've been through but you damn sure can show people how they can grow through it. Come walk and grown with me Queens. Let's all tell our stories and unite as one. I did it and so can you.

Made in the USA
Monee, IL
17 August 2020

38745766R00066